GHOST STORIES
of the OLD SOUTH

Edrick Thay

GHOST HOUSE

Ghost House Books

The Publisher: Ghost House Books
Distributed by Lone Pine Publishing
10145 – 81 Avenue
Edmonton, AB, Canada T6E 1W9
Website: http://www.ghostbooks.net

1808 – B Street NW, Suite 140
Auburn, WA, USA 98001

National Library of Canada Cataloguing in Publication Data

Thay, Edrick, 1977–
    Ghost stories of the Old South / Edrick Thay.

    ISBN 1-894877-18-7
    1. Ghosts—Southern States. 2. Legends—Southern States. I. Title.
GR108.T42 2003   398.2'097505   C2003-910281-5

Editorial Director: Nancy Foulds
Editorial: Shelagh Kubish
Illustrations Coordinator: Carol Woo
Production Manager: Gene Longson
Cover Design: Gerry Dotto
Layout & Production: Jeff Fedorkiw
Photo Credits: Every effort has been made to accurately credit photographers. Any errors or omissions should be directed to the publisher for changes in future editions. The photographs and illustrations in this book are reproduced with the kind permission of the following sources: Library of Congress (p. 11: HABS, TENN,19-NASH,1-4; p. 9, 13: HABS, TENN,19-NASH,1-2; p. 15: HABS, TENN,19-NASH,1-5; p. 22: HABS, NC,92-RAL,5-2; p. 30: HABS, GA,26-SAV,24-3; p. 33: HABS, GA,26-SAV,24-5; p. 45: USZ62-87798; p. 48: USZ62-117931; p. 65: HABS, MISS,44-COLUM,14-1; p. 95, 106: HABS, MISS,44-COLUM.V,2-2; p. 109: HABS, MISS,44-COLUM.V,2-3; p. 126: HABS, VA,19-WEST.1-9; p. 3, 129: HABS, VA,19-WEST.1-61; p. 133: HABS, VA,19-WEST,1-5; p. 148: HABS, ALA,24-SEL,1-1; p. 151: HABS, ALA,24-SEL,1-7; p. 146, 153: HABS, FLA,55-SAUG,1-14; p. 156: HABS, FLA,55-SAUG, 1-39; p. 159: HAER, TENN,78-GAT.V,6I-4; p. 183: HABS,MISS,45-MAND,1-1; p. 4-5, 175 189: HABS,SC,10-CHAR,306-1; p. 194: HABS, LA,36-NEWOR,18-8; p. 196: HABS, LA,36-NEWOR,18-13; p. 198: HABS, LA,36-NEWOR,18-10), Eyewire (p. 120), New Orleans Public Library, Louisiana Division (p. 141: C. Milo Williams Photograph Collection; p. 144: Louisiana Photograph Collection), Okefenokee Adventures/Joy Campbell (p. 163, 165).

We acknowledge the financial support of the Government of Canada through the Book Publishing Industry Development Program (BPIDP) for our publishing activities.

PC: P6

To Johnny Blaze (the original Gamecock),
David Zimmer and Andrea Dilliner

Contents

Acknowledgments

There are many people to thank for helping to make this collection of words into something tangible and coherent.

Alana Bevan deserves many thanks for her hours of research.

Shelagh Kubish deserves many thanks for her patient editing.

Carol Woo deserves many thanks for her ability to supply the images that bring life to the words.

Ghost House's production staff deserves many thanks for making this book look good.

Nancy Foulds deserves many thanks for her advice.

Shane Kennedy deserves many thanks for giving me this opportunity.

Ghost story writers from all over the South deserve more than just thanks for carving out the trail I followed. Writers such as Nancy Roberts, Kathryn Windham, L.B. Taylor, Jr., and Dennis William Hauck have done so much for the Southern ghost story that this collection pales in comparison.

And finally, a thanks to all those who provided me with encouragement and support throughout the writing of this text. I need not mention their names, for they know who they are.

Introduction

This project wasn't meant to be about the South of Flannery O'Connor or Tennessee Williams or William Faulkner, but the South that existed before the Civil War, the South that embodied the contradictions of human existence in a society where men were gentlemen, women were belles and society was civilized and enlightened. Underneath that veneer, of course, existed slavery, where blacks, taken from their homes in Africa, were sold as property and shackled as slaves. Slavery was not specific to the agricultural South, but with the approach of the Civil War, the two became synonymous. It's an unfair view, of course, and the United States as a whole still struggles with its guilt over the centuries-long reliance on the practice.

However, the antebellum South was not composed solely of plantations and their crops of cotton and tobacco. As I sifted through the stories of ghost hunters such as Nancy Roberts, Kathryn Windham and L.B. Taylor, Jr., it became clear that the antebellum South was a diverse world, with a number of identities and personalities. There were the pirates of Georgia and New Orleans, buccaneers upon whom the sun had not yet set. There were the revolutionaries who banded together to fight the British and gain a country of their own. There were the architects who designed and erected the grand and regal domes of such cities as Raleigh and Atlanta. There were natural phenomena that mystified Indian tribes and European explorers, phenomena that continue to baffle the rational and scientific minds of the 21st century.

The Old South is a world that still exists in some parts, whether as an idea or as a restoration of the past through the preservation of historically important buildings. It is a world that still exists in folklore and story, preserved, like artifacts, in the ghost stories that have been passed down from generation to generation like heirlooms. It is a world that still exists because it should not be forgotten. Take these stories as a snapshot of human consciousness, Polaroids of the creation, development and evolution of a nation. Take them, as I did, as a passport to a different time and a different place.

1
Phantoms in Public

That's Dedication
NASHVILLE, TENNESSEE

When legislators in Nashville decided that the small house where they met to govern the affairs of the state of Tennessee was inadequate for their purposes, they asked architects all across the country to submit proposals for a new state capitol. Despite competition from architects such as Adolphus Heiman, who had already designed several admired structures throughout the state, William Strickland won the contract. There was fierce opposition to the choice. Heiman was a great architect who had made his home in Tennessee, while Strickland was from the industrial North, an area that strove to extinguish the South and its distinct way of life, and had worked mostly in the northeast.

Despite the initial resistance, Strickland managed to find a place for himself in both Tennessee history and consciousness. The man from the northeast, who some hail as one of America's greatest early architects, has become inexorably linked to the Tennessee State Capitol. In fact, Strickland moved to Nashville when he received the contract and lived there for nine years before dying. His body was interred within the state capitol and even now, over a century and a half after his death in 1854, he can still be seen walking the halls of the state capitol, his testament to Greek design and classicism.

William Strickland arrived in Nashville in 1845, with plans for a building 232 feet by 124 feet, with a surrounding terrace, a Doric basement, four Ionic porticoes and a Corinthian tower in the center of the roof. His designs

The Tennessee State Capitol in Nashville, designed by the celebrated architect—and ghost—William Strickland

resonated so strongly with Tennesseans that public buildings throughout the state were erected with Strickland's designs in mind. The irony, of course, is that the building that continues to be the source of much inspiration and pride was, for its creator, the source of far too much aggravation and frustration.

While the cornerstone for the building was laid on July 4, 1845, bureaucratic conflicts hampered the building's construction, delaying its completion for nine years. The project had started and stalled a number of times, usually because funds were depleted, but more often because Strickland became enraged with the man chosen to oversee his work, Samuel Morgan. Handpicked by the Capitol Commission, Samuel Morgan was a willful man who would not relent on his decisions. It was his job to keep Strickland under budget, and to do so, he initiated a number of arguments over building materials, labor costs and, most insulting of all, design concerns. Strickland saw Morgan as a man who understood little about art, while Morgan saw Strickland as someone prone to flights of fancy and with little regard for the state's budget. Yet Strickland persevered, all the while seemingly aware of his own mortality. Why else would he have designed a vault in the capitol's north wall with instructions to inter his body there upon his death?

During lulls in construction or when he needed a break from the politics of his work on the state capitol, Strickland designed grand mansions inspired by Italian villas, and the First Presbyterian Church, with its Egyptian influences. He died on April 7, 1854, and while the capitol had been in use since 1853, the structure had yet to be completed. Strickland's son, Francis, oversaw the completion of the building. The final stone was finally put in place on July 21, 1855. When completed, the capitol had indeed become everything that Strickland had first envisioned. For all of Morgan's stubbornness, Strickland's vision was realized, save for one little wrinkle. When Morgan

Strickland's elaborate plans for the building often conflicted with those of Samuel Morgan, his supervisor.

died, fate seized upon his passing as an opportunity to offer up one of its infamous twists.

Coincidentally, Morgan was interred within the north wall alongside Strickland. The enmity that existed between the two in life has not abated in death. Even with the debacle of the capitol's construction behind them, the two have been unable to forgive or forget and continue to bicker and squabble well into their afterlives. The capitol is often the scene of heated debate and conflict as state legislators attempt to determine how best to serve the people; however, the building usually falls silent after bags have been packed and rooms cleared for the evening. Or so security guards hired to patrol the grounds would have thought.

Patrolling the grounds late one evening, a guard stopped abruptly outside the capitol. He stood by a window, sifting through the sounds of traffic and the night trying to make sense of what he'd heard. Somewhere beneath the hum of traffic, he heard voices. The building was empty, that much he knew. He had just completed a tour of its halls and when he was inside, all he had heard was the echoing of his footsteps down the deserted hallways. But now, it sounded as if a heated argument were taking place. Given the facts, how could that be?

A quick look around the capitol revealed that all its doors were still locked, ruling out the possibility of an intruder. Unsure of what he could do on his own, he placed a call to the police department, asking them to investigate the noise. Officers arrived and searched the capitol, but found nothing. An officer familiar with the capitol giggled. He knew what the security guard was seeking, having spent many a dark night in the empty capitol.

The guard found the officer's suppressed laughter upsetting and demanded to know what was so amusing. The police officer explained, detailing to the guard how Nashville came to have its capitol building and two

*Security guards have heard ghostly voices arguing in the halls—
probably Strickland and Morgan, still squabbling in the afterlife.*

ghosts besides. The security guard stared at the officer,
incredulous.

"Just wait," the officer said. "You'll be a believer yet."

The more the security guard worked at the capitol, the
more he became convinced that the officer had been telling
the truth. There was something strange about the building.
He heard the two strident voices ringing throughout the
halls often and began to see that the arguments always took

place around the north wall. When the guard asked a superior who had been working at the capitol for years why that seemed to be the case, the superior replied as if the answer were obvious.

"Hey, it's where those two boys are buried, Strickland and Morgan. They're both in there." Strickland and Morgan are still in the wall, still squabbling over their visions for the Tennessee State Capitol, both forever enshrined in the same building. That's dedication.

Lucas Tavern
MONTGOMERY, ALABAMA

If only I had a guide to pose for me, the photographer thought as he set up a tripod to take photographs. He had secured permission to stay in Old Alabama Town in Montgomery past closing but had forgotten to ask one of the historical guides to stay behind. The shots he planned to take in the one-room schoolhouse would have had far more immediacy if there'd been a model pretending to be a 19th-century teacher. He sighed. It was still nice to be in the historic district, with its collection of restored and preserved buildings dating from the 1820s. The work that preservationists had done here was incredible; painstaking research and work had resulted in the creation of a living museum populated with historical interpreters to usher visitors back in time. As he set up in the fading light, peering through his camera's viewfinder with the creaking of the wooden floorboards echoing around him in the classroom, he paused. He looked up and saw in front of him a guide, a woman dressed in the fashion of the 19th century, posing by the window with a *McGuffey Reader* in her hand.

The photographer began taking pictures, grateful that one of the museum's staff had chosen to stay behind and pose for him. He snapped away and then decided to change angles. As he picked up his tripod, he bumped one of its legs into a desk, sending a loud crack through the air. The sound startled the woman, and she began to walk towards the door. Worried that his subject was abandoning him, the photographer implored the guide not to leave. Without a word, the guide moved silently and came to a stop beneath a portrait of George Washington. There, she turned to face the photographer, staring at him with eyes that bore into his soul. He began shivering, rubbing his arms and stamping his feet to keep warm even though the day was hot and humid, a typical Montgomery summer day. Then he watched with amazement and shock as the woman turned and walked through the wall. With her disappearance, the room grew warm once again and the photographer was left to wonder what exactly he had seen.

How fortuitous, he thought, that he had taken photographs of the woman. The first thing he did the next morning was develop the film. Standing in his darkroom, he gasped as image after image of the classroom materialized to show not the woman he had seen in the hoop skirt and tight corset, but instead, a brilliant golden light. He returned to the Old Town Visitor Center where he showed the photographs to a guide. She nodded knowingly and smiled.

"How wonderful," she said. "You've just met Eliza Lucas."

The photographer knew then that the stories he'd heard about the hauntings in Montgomery's historic district were true. There really was a spirit named Eliza Lucas who made sure that visits to Old Town were memorable.

Lucas Tavern was built in the early 19th century to accommodate the number of travelers who passed through Montgomery. The tavern owners prided themselves on providing the best the South had to offer, and it was women like Eliza who lent credence to the idea of Southern hospitality. The tavern was known for catering to the upscale traveler, and its guests included the Marquis de Lafayette, a general and a hero of the American Revolution, who stayed there on his way to New Orleans.

While he stayed only a night, Lafayette was said to have been impressed enough to recall the experience in great detail to friends, lauding Eliza's chicken pie, ham and fried vegetables and the hearty breakfast of grits, eggs, biscuits and gravy and sausage. It wasn't long before travelers began staying at the Lucas Tavern as much for Eliza's cooking as for her gracious hospitality. Her reputation as a caring and attentive hostess ensured that guests would return again and again and that new ones would arrive on the strength of recommendations. Eliza was a simple woman, her background ordinary, her education limited. But she was known and respected as a woman with an unparalleled strength of heart and character. She worked to make sure that visitors always had a warm, comfortable and clean place to rest, and that they left with the desire to return.

Eliza died before she saw the nation split apart in the battles of the Civil War. Her husband continued to run the tavern, but he died soon after. The two are buried in the Old Augusta Cemetery about three miles from their tavern. A succession of owners came and went before conservation-minded individuals decided to preserve a collection of 19th-century buildings, among them, the Lucas Tavern. Restorations were completed in 1979, and the Lucas Tavern, which opened up onto the square of historical buildings, was chosen to serve as a Visitor's Reception Center and as the offices of Old Alabama Town. A year later, people began noting that the restorations had brought back to life not only the building, but also its most famous resident, Eliza Lucas.

As the Visitor Center, the Lucas Tavern was subject to the comings and goings of pedestrians around Old Alabama Town. For Eliza, the particular rhythm of the building must have felt like a calling to return to her hosting duties, and the building was once again a symbol of Montgomery. The restoration of the square has agreed with her disposition, and it is not just the tavern that she frequents. As the photographer discovered, Eliza has made a habit of touring the historic buildings that must remind her of her life in Montgomery. Old Alabama Town, then, has achieved its ultimate goal to recapture and reanimate the past; after all, how better to gauge their success than by watching Eliza Lucas' reactions? By all accounts, she is thrilled and wants nothing more than to guarantee visitors the best experience possible. When she's not waving hello to guests, she's inside the various buildings, rearranging furniture and knickknacks.

She also appears at board meetings, and staff and guides feel she is a kind and gentle spirit whose presence is helpful and informative. People can still remember the time that a committee meeting became heated. One member became irate, raising his voice and rising to his feet to emphasize his point. As he pointed his finger at his colleagues, a cloud of ash blew from the fireplace, covering him in soot. He stood there, blinking his eyes and coughing, then excused himself from the room. There are proper ways to carry yourself, Eliza seemed to be saying, and made sure that the committee member knew the errors of his ways. She expressed her displeasure in other ways as well, dropping a door from its hinges and bringing it crashing down to the floor when two guides were complaining about their work in Old Alabama Town. They found other things to talk about.

Although Eliza Lucas died over 140 years ago, her love for the community has survived, fostering the growth and development of a city that has grown from a town of several hundred people to a city with over 200,000 inhabitants. Surely she could claim some small credit for Montgomery's early growth, when travelers first became acquainted with the city when they stayed at the Lucas Tavern. Now, she has returned to once again remind people exactly what Southern hospitality is.

Talk About a Filibuster
RALEIGH, NORTH CAROLINA

The North Carolina State Capitol is known as one of the best-preserved and finest examples of the Greek Revival style of architecture. Many of the nation's government buildings in the early 19th century duplicated this style, following the lead established in Washington, D.C., with its monumental public buildings. The North Carolina State Capitol is not the largest or even the grandest building of its kind, but there are few such buildings in the United States that can rival this capitol's preservation. Much of the building appears as it did when its doors were first opened for public service in 1840. The stonework, ornamental plaster and ironwork, the mahogany desks and chairs gracing the various offices and all but one of the marble mantels are original; they have not been restored or replaced with reproductions. The capitol is almost perfectly preserved, as if it had been plucked from 1840 and transported to the 21st century.

Little surprise, then, that along with the furnishings and ornaments, spirits of the past are living in this building as well. The General Assembly moved to the State Legislature Building in 1963, leaving the governor and lieutenant governor as the capitol's only tenants, but the capitol still sees its share of political squabbling. Long-dead politicians who had once served their state in the capitol have not let death prevent them from continuing to do so.

At the end of the American Revolution, Raleigh was little more than an idea and a blueprint. It consisted of

The identity of the spirit inside North Carolina's old State Capitol remains a mystery.

just a few streets that wended their way around five public squares. But the fledgling legislature decided to erect a small and rather plain building there in 1796 to serve their governmental needs. In 1822, political leaders had the building upgraded, but by 1831, a clumsy construction worker accidentally set the building ablaze.

In December 1832, the legislature agreed to appropriate $50,000 for the construction of a new capitol on the same site. This time, no expense would be spared in the capitol's construction; legislators were determined to give North Carolinians something that few of them had ever seen: "a noble monument" that they could call their own and claim as an object of "just and becoming pride." The General Assembly asked that plans for the new capitol expand upon the old State House—that is, plans needed to incorporate a cross-shaped building with a central, domed rotunda. For the building's design, the state settled on plans submitted by the New York architectural firm of Ithiel Town and Alexander Jackson. The choice was obvious; the firm was known for its Greek Revival influence, embodied most visibly by the public buildings of Washington, D.C. Town and Jackson had just completed the Connecticut State Capitol in New Haven and were hard at work in Indianapolis to design the Hoosier State's capitol.

The remains of the old State House were cleared away and on the Fourth of July, 1833, construction on the new capitol began. Work was slow and halting, as funds were exhausted time and time again. Little wonder that money was spent quickly; artisans from as far as Scotland were hired to work on the capitol, while ironwork, chandeliers and other hardware came from Philadelphia. But as the building began to take shape, the full scope of Town and Jackson's vision became apparent and the money became secondary. When the building was finished in 1840, seven years had passed and $533,000 had been spent. Its cost was more than 3.5 times the state's total revenue for that year.

When the doors of the capitol were opened to a curious public, any misgivings the people might have had were dispelled. The awe and wonder in the eyes of those gazing upon the capitol's magnificence told designers and the state that in the capitol, they had created a treasure.

It was originally designed for use by all offices of the state department, including the Supreme Court, the governor and the General Assembly. With so many offices and so many different people moving about over so many years, it's not surprising that the capitol has become a reservoir not only of history but also of personalities. In time, though, the state departments grew too unwieldy to be housed in just one building. The Supreme Court and State Library moved into their own building in 1888, while the General Assembly began meeting in the new State Legislative Building in 1963. Only the governor and the lieutenant governor remained in the building. Or so they thought.

A night watchman named Mr. Jackson had worked in the capitol building for 15 years. During most of that time, his nights were quiet and uneventful. He believed that once the capitol housed only the governor and the lieutenant governor, the place would be as still and silent as a morgue. In a strange and unexpected way, Jackson was right. There were people who had spent most of their lives in the capitol, devoting their time and energies to their work in the hopes of bettering the state of North Carolina. Their dedication seemed to reach beyond their lives and into death.

Jackson's nightly rounds became the setting for a symphony of the supernatural. As he walked the wide halls, nightstick at his side and flashlight in hand, he would stop and turn his attention to a door behind him. He wondered how he could hear it slam just moments after he had passed it and locked it. Was there someone in the building? He tried the door, but it was still locked. Maybe someone was hiding inside. He unlocked the door and rushed through the doorway. But the room was empty. He then confirmed that he was the only person in the building.

Another time, Jackson was walking by the library when he heard books falling from the bookcases. He'd heard them drop three times, loud and clear. Yet when he searched the library, when the overhead light had dispelled the gloom and restored the warmth of the dark wooden bookcases, he saw nothing amiss. The floor was clear of any obstruction. What, then, had he heard, if no books had dropped to the ground? As the nights wore on and the events acquired a predictability and familiarity about them, Jackson found himself becoming accustomed to the paranormal.

He still marveled at how the manually operated elevator could travel from floor to floor with no one in it. He no longer cursed the air after he had run up two flights of stairs in response to what sounded like breaking glass only to find everything untouched and unbroken. Always, he found the panes of glass whole and all windows into the building securely locked. He no longer jumped out of his seat when he felt a cold hand on his neck; instead, he nodded and smiled before turning back to his work. Anytime something strange and unusual happened, Jackson would sigh and just attribute the actions to "the saint."

Sam Townsend had worked as an administrator at the capitol and liked to work late into the evening at least three times a week. Work during the day was fraught with distractions, and Townsend preferred the quiet of the night and the emptiness of the building when doing the bulk of his work. But then he began to understand what it was that Jackson had been talking about all those times the watchman had come to him, wide-eyed and shaken.

One night, Townsend was in his office working when he heard someone walking down the hall from the committee room toward his little office. The footsteps were loud and seemed to be right outside his door. He opened the door and immediately the footsteps stopped. All Townsend could hear was the humming of his fan. The hallway was empty. He looked up one end of the hall and then the other but there was no mistaking that he was alone. The hallway wasn't the only place where Townsend was subjected to the mysterious footsteps. In the committee room, Townsend heard footsteps pacing back and forth across the floor. There were times when he was in the room and would hear the steps, yet never once did he see anyone walking across the floor. Perhaps frightened off by technology, the footsteps stopped when a copier was stored in the room temporarily. But the footsteps returned when the copier was moved from the room and into another office.

But lest one fret that the apparition chooses to remain only heard and unseen, Townsend explains that the apparition, while shy, has been known to make an occasional appearance. Townsend came to the capitol one evening to work and opened the door to the Senate chamber, curious to listen for the footsteps that had become as much a part of his routine as his two cups of black coffee with just a bit of sugar. A surprise was waiting for him.

When he opened the door to the Senate chamber, a figure was standing in the doorway. He stepped back in fright; he'd thought he was alone. And then, he watched in silent amazement as the figure before him, less a being than a shadow, faded from sight, like a Polaroid in reverse. Townsend was left standing in the light of the Senate chamber with nothing but his lonely shadow behind him for company.

Raymond Beck, a curator for the building in 1981, was also working late when he encountered the apparition of the capitol. He was in the library on the third floor, doing some research and other related work. He sat at his desk, taking notes while his tiny transistor radio played in the background. Finished with some books that he taken down from the shelves, Beck walked over to the shelves to replace them. But then they fell from his hands. He heard the dull thud of the books against the ground and he turned to see who was behind him. Only there was nobody there. Just rows of books cast in shadow and light. Still, Beck was positive he had felt someone's icy grip upon his shoulder, felt eyes boring into his back, and felt a growing sense of discomfort and anxiety. But the library was empty and when he called out to see if anyone was there, he heard only the echo of his own voice. Beck bent down, urgency in his actions, and picked up the books and with a couple of quick glances down at their spines was able to put them quickly where they belonged. He felt the overwhelming urge to flee. He gathered up his papers and his bag and left the library. His work was finished for the evening.

Visitors have reported hearing pistol shots outside the building and screams echoing throughout the stands of oak trees that were planted near the capitol so many years ago. The location was once popular with duelists, when dueling was still accepted by true Southern gentlemen as the only means of settling a dispute under the eyes of the Lord.

It's difficult to know exactly who it is that continues to haunt the capitol. So many arguments were borne out there, as were so many lives, that there must be any number of souls who want to continue being part of the historic building.

Because It's Cold Out
SAVANNAH, GEORGIA

Joseph Habersham, Jr., native son of Savannah, Georgia, was born into a fiercely Loyalist family with a patriarch who could only watch with disgust and indignation when his sons joined the fight for independence in the American Revolution. The fires of war often become the forge within which the mettle of men is tempered and proven; Habersham, Jr., thrived in the American Revolution.

Educated at Princeton, he returned to his home state where he began to recruit youth to the independence movement. He helped organize the "Liberty Boys," a group of radical patriots who wanted British rule abolished. Habersham became a colonel in the Continental Army, served in the Continental Congress and was a member of the Georgia Convention that ratified the Constitution of the United States. It's even said that the Declaration of Independence had its first public reading in Habersham's house. On January 17, 1776, Habersham led a band of men and captured and arrested Atlanta's British Colonial Governor, Sir James Wright. After the war, Habersham served at various times as mayor of Savannah, the United States Postmaster General under Presidents Washington, Adams and Jefferson, and in the last years of his life, as president of the Georgia branch of the Bank of the United States. Habersham died in 1815. Just three years later, in recognition of his contributions to the country as well as the state, Georgian

The old Pink House in Savannah, Georgia

legislators named Habersham County in his honor. Savannah's citizens are grateful to Habersham for another reason, though—one that has nothing to do with politics.

Habersham lived in Savannah in a Georgian-style mansion he had built at 23 Abercorn Street in 1771. Thomas Jefferson is believed to have had a hand in its design. In the early 19th century, Habersham had the house expanded when it was renovated to become the headquarters for the Planter's Bank, the first such institution in the state of Georgia. In the basement, he placed the vault. And while it was a bank and a home, folks knew the house for completely different reasons.

Originally cast in white stucco, Habersham's house acquired a different hue as the years wore on. Underneath the white was red brick, whose coloring leached through the stucco, rendering the once-dazzling white home a very odd and very peculiar pink. Washington, D.C., might have the White House, but Savannah has the Pink House, the name by which Habersham's house became known. The house seems particularly blessed, despite its color and the ridicule Habersham suffered for it. When the great fire of 1796 swept through the city, claiming two-thirds of its historic buildings, the Pink House was one of the few homes to escape unscathed. It endeared itself to the city, a symbol of persistence and triumph over adversity, of Savannah's strength and resilience.

For the last 50 years, the Pink House has served fine Southern cuisine, earning a reputation as one of Savannah's best restaurants and the only one to serve its meals amid the splendor of an 18th-century home. Its food is warmly received, but what draws some people here is an item that cannot be found on the menu alongside crab cakes, stuffed grouper and pork tenderloin.

Some people come to eat at the Pink House because its original owner and builder, James Habersham, Jr., is still there enjoying the comforts of his historic home. It's not known why exactly, but between the months of October and March, Habersham returns to the restaurant. What he does for the rest of the year is a mystery, but perhaps he comes indoors because he is not a fan of cold weather.

Habersham may have been, from the outside, a successful and determined gentleman, but who knows what sorts of thoughts and ideas lurked beneath the surface? His must have been a personality torn apart with doubt, insecurity and fear, for despite the outward trappings of success, one evening he walked down to the basement, opened the steel bank vault door and hanged himself from the ceiling. Bank employees found his body when they wondered about the rapping sound at the vault door. It was his feet, knocking against the steel. People later discovered that he suspected his wife, Mary Bolton, of having an affair; the shame of being cuckolded seemed too much to bear.

Bartenders now often allege that their bar is a favorite for one particular man, a strange yet well-dressed man who looked very much as if he had stepped out of the 18th century and into the 21st. When the bartenders notice him, he is always perched upon the same chair, sipping from a glass of Madeira. His eyes move throughout the room, stopping at each table to reflect and watch the guests.

"Who is that?" the uninitiated whisper, half-pointing at the man. "Who served him?"

*James Habersham, the ghost of the Pink House, is pleased when guests
enjoy their visit to his former home.*

It's then that they learn that it is none other than James
Habersham, Jr., sipping the Madeira upon which some
of the family's fortunes were built. The belief is that
Habersham, ever the considerate and gracious host,
approves of what has been done with his house and
appears to guests by way of greeting and to make sure that

everything is running as smoothly as possible and that guests have a memorable visit. Habersham is enormously proud of his home still, and as its owner and Georgian patriot, he has every reason to celebrate a triumphant return to the Pink House.

Of course, no one seems to know why he is busiest between the months of October to May. During the summer months, Habersham is rarely seen, and when he is, it's in the candles that illuminate themselves as if lit by unseen hands. Like Persephone, who could walk the earth for only six months a year, Habersham frequents the inn for only a brief period of time. Perhaps when the air is hot and humid, he prefers to be outside where he can be refreshed and rejuvenated. In the colder months, he takes comfort in the smiles of men and women, enjoying the camaraderie.

Strange Bedfellows
RALEIGH, NORTH CAROLINA

People can be quite particular about the smallest things. One person takes only cream in his coffee, another wants it black. Preferences are extensions of personality, symbols of the individual. Little surprise, then, that the dead often return with the same particular likes and dislikes that distinguished them in life. These preferences can cause problems when they differ from changes made to the spirits' former homes.

In 1883, Governor Thomas Jarvis passed a bill allowing for construction of a new official governor's residence on Burke Square in Raleigh. Executive Mansion was completed in 1891, and the first governor to live in it was Daniel Fowle. North Carolina's current governor lives in the mansion, and tours of the first floor are available to the public. A visit to the home will reveal inscriptions on the bricks used in construction and the names of prison inmates who molded the bricks. The house also contains elegant marble staircases and beautiful oak and heart pine lumber.

The two architects responsible for the design and building of Executive Mansion were Samuel Sloan and Aldophus Gustavus Bauer. Sloan, who had been responsible for the bulk of the plans, did not live to see his plans come to fruition. He died in 1885, leaving Bauer to shoulder the burden of the mansion's completion. Bauer followed Sloan's plans faithfully, incorporating the spacious halls, reception rooms and 16-foot ceilings. The mansion was completed after years of financial wrangling and debate and included 15 rooms, with a gentleman's parlor, ballroom, library, dining room, ladies parlor and a morning room. Handmade rugs decorated the gentleman's parlor; handmade bookcases from Asheville showcased an impressive book collection in the library.

Although years have passed and some changes have been made to the interior, its exterior has remained much the same, still bearing the steeply pitched gable, patterned chimneys and elaborate woodwork that so awed and dazzled the public when the mansion was finished in 1891. The largest room in the house serves as a dining room, whose centerpiece is a San Domingo mahogany table around which up to 24 people can eat and converse in supreme opulence. Providing light is a grand Austrian chandelier donated at the close of the Second World War by a German woman impressed with North Carolina hospitality.

When Jeanelle C. Moore occupied the house for four years beginning in 1965 as the state's First Lady, she felt a need to protect the home so that future generations might enjoy it as much as she had. Under her leadership, a public campaign was mounted to educate the public about the mansion's place in both culture and history. Her efforts resulted in the formation of the Executive Mansion Fine Arts Committee, which advises and funds the acquisition of gifts, maintenance and preservation. Partly because of Moore's efforts, the National Register of Historic Places added the mansion to its list in 1970. The Executive Mansion Fund, formed in 1988, ensures that the mansion will remain a treasure for generations. One person in particular—Daniel Fowle—must surely be happy with the building's status as a state treasure. The mansion's first occupant, Fowle continues to play an active role in the mansion's maintenance, though he has been dead for many years.

Daniel Fowle was so taken with his new home that he moved his family in even before interior designers had a chance to furnish the mansion. To help expedite the process and guarantee his comfort, Fowle submitted plans for the construction and installation of a massive wooden bed to the finest carpenters and craftsmen North Carolina had to offer. The bed was unlike any other—Fowle was exacting and demanding in what he wanted, and when completed, it was less a bed than an extension of the governor's tastes. Fowle's time in the mansion, however, was brief. He moved in on January 5, 1891, and died three months later, on April 7.

For years, governors came and went, all using Fowle's bed. Perhaps they deemed its move to another room too massive an undertaking, or maybe they liked the old wooden bed—the way it connected the present with the past, handed down, like the house, from governor to governor. Whatever the reason, the bed lay undisturbed for almost 90 years, until Governor Bob Scott moved into the house in 1970.

Scott tried sleeping in the bed, but there was something about it that just made lying in it too uncomfortable. Old and weathered, the bed emitted loud piercing squeaks whenever Scott climbed into, moved around on, or got out of the bed. After a succession of sleepless nights, Scott decided that he would break with tradition and use a bed of his own. He had movers carefully disassemble the bed and cart its pieces for reassembly into a little used third-floor bedroom. Scott bought a more modern king-size bed. Unfortunately, Scott still did not find the rest that he was seeking.

Certainly, a creaking bed frame was no longer the problem, but now he was roused from slumber by a rapping sound that seemed to come from just above his head. Scott turned on the lamp and looked up at the wall. The sound was still audible and growing louder. He got out of bed and walked into the next room to see if someone from his family was knocking on the wall. But there was no one there. The house had fallen into darkness and the air itself was heavy with slumber. He returned to his bed where the knocking persisted, having become more insistent in his absence. Scott was at a loss as to what to do. He couldn't help noticing that the strange sound seemed to be coming from the spot where Fowle's bed headboard used to rest against the wall.

The next morning, Scott awoke feeling significantly less refreshed than he had hoped. He'd finally fallen asleep late into the evening after the knocking had subsided. He wasn't aware of the time, just of the growing frustration and gnawing anxiety that accompanies sleepless nights.

For the next four years, the knocking in Scott's bedroom continued night after night. Thinking it could be no one other than Fowle, Scott's family attributed the disturbances to the spirit they christened Governor Fowle's Ghost. But Scott refused to relinquish his bed. In time, he grew accustomed to Fowle's nightly presence and never once considered moving Fowle's bed back to the second-floor bedroom.

In 1974, Scott's term ended and a new governor moved into the Executive Mansion. He moved Fowle's bed to the second-floor bedroom and, eerily enough, Fowle was never heard from again. Since that time, the governors appear to have learned from Governor Scott's experience. Twenty-seven governors have lived in the house now, and only one is believed to have reported an encounter with the ghost. Bob Scott wanted his own bed, not Fowle's. Fowle disagreed, apparently feeling that his bed had become an immutable part of the Executive Mansion's legacy, as valuable and important to the house's history as its Queen Anne style of Victorian architecture. Or maybe Fowle was extremely particular about the placement of his bed. Moving it was perhaps an insult to his taste and personality. Those who disagree with Fowle's placement of the bed are invited to move it—at their own risk.

Shivering Timbers
SAVANNAH, GEORGIA

Once upon a time, there was a garden. In this garden, colonists led by General Oglethorpe sowed the seeds of what they hoped would be prosperity. In this experimental garden, crops from all over the known world were planted in 10 acres with the hope that some or all of them would flourish and thus provide the fledgling colony of Savannah with the means necessary to secure a future. Eventually, peach trees grew strong and tall, and cotton grew successfully as well. Here, on the sunny banks of the Savannah River, Savannah took root, breathing life into the state of Georgia.

By 1753, the experimental garden was no longer needed. The land was seized by entrepreneurs who saw their futures not in the earth, but in the hordes of sailors who helped make Savannah a thriving port city. And so begins the tale of the Pirates' House, an inn of such ill repute and notoriety that it is easy to forget that it was built on a garden, where life springs eternal. Tales of the Pirates' House were many, but all had at their hearts a common theme: the lawlessness of men and the possibility for corruption from within. Some guests of the Pirates' House were so infamous that they have never been forgotten. Indeed, some of them have never even left.

In the 18th century, the inn was not a place for the faint of heart; it was a rough-and-tumble place where only the hardest and most emboldened men dared to tread. Inside, amid the dim candlelight obscured by pipe smoke, the sweet sickly smell of rum and sweat mingled with the mixture of heavy, thick accents as sailors and pirates from all over the world gathered to hash and rehash their legendary tales of bravado. Men came to the inn from China, India, Africa, South America and Europe for rest and a warm meal.

As it was a meeting place of the damned, the law frequented the establishment often, eager to seek out an arrest or a bribe. But the pirates developed their own brand of evasion. Out on the high seas, there was no law, and policemen were helpless to stop them. A tunnel had been built in the cellar of the inn, leading to the river and the harbor. Unsuspecting policemen were often drugged and then carried into the tunnel to waiting ships where their slumbering bodies were shipped to destinations across the globe. Legend tells of a policeman who awoke to find himself on his way to China. After being taken to Shanghai, it took him two years to find his way back to Georgia. Sailors were not immune to this sort of treatment; everyone was fair game and captains looking to replace men lost at sea through scurvy or other means often drugged men who refused a first solicitation and then put them to work on their ships.

Although the Pirates' House is now a friendly dining establishment, every effort has been made to preserve its unique atmosphere. Little of the architecture has been changed and diners can still gaze up at the same hand-hewn ceiling beams joined with wooden pegs that have seen and heard everything. Even with all the amenities of a 21st-century building, the Pirates' House still has an atmosphere and allure all its own. It helps, of course, that buccaneer ghosts still frequent the inn; brigands of the high seas like Jean Lafitte and Captain Flint called the inn home for stretches at a time, and some locals believe that these pirates still do.

Captain Flint is believed to have died in the inn. Crippled with an illness that the medicine of the day could not cure, Flint just wanted to numb his pain and die in peace. As he lay in bed, Flint stared feebly at the ceiling. Parched, he longed for a drink. Water wouldn't do. It would have to be something stronger, far more intoxicating. He wanted to escape and, as he clutched his blanket, he called out for his first mate, Darby McGraw.

"Rum," he croaked. "Bring me some rum, McGraw."

When his first mate didn't move fast enough, he called out again, "Rum, dammit. And be quick about it. I might be dyin', but there's strength enough still in these arms to raise my saber. I want more rum. Darby, bring aft the rum."

As the liquor trickled its way down Flint's throat, he felt a warm flush work its way across his body. He gulped greedily, sucking down the dregs of the bottle Darby had brought.

"Aye, that's good. One more, Darby. Bring aft the rum."

Darby looked into his captain's eyes, and in the inky black of Flint's pupils, he could see life ebbing away.

"I'm dyin', boy. Rum, dammit. Rum."

Flint died in the upstairs bedroom days later but still, restaurant goers and staff claim that on nights when the sky is clear but the land is dark, Flint returns from the grave. He walks the tunnel beneath the restaurant, a large, lumbering scar-faced apparition. In his day, Flint must have walked the route more than once, carrying out either sailors or policemen. Upstairs, in the room where Flint died, his last days are reenacted as his ghost continues to call for Darby McGraw to bring him his rum. Many diners have been startled by the raspy call for the liquor, often looking right then left, wondering if someone in the restaurant could be so rude. When enlightened with the truth, many of them simply scratch their heads, stare up at the ceiling, smile, and go back to their food. If Captain Flint is going to stay at the inn, who is going to be bold enough to evict him? The restaurant is, after all, called the Pirates' House. With a name like that, little wonder that here in Savannah the past is alive and well.

Sword Gate
CHARLESTON, SOUTH CAROLINA

Madame Talvande wanted the best for the girls placed in her charge at Madame Talvande's French School for Young Ladies. Parents trusted her with the education and upbringing of their young daughters and turned to her to instill in their children the values and morals that all proper ladies should heed and respect. Over 100 girls were in her care at any given time, many from an early age. And while Talvande could be caring and gentle, when she lost her temper, she became a vicious harpy bent and twisted with cruelty. According to Mary Chesnut, who wrote an autobiographical account called *Two Years, or the Way We Lived Then*, in 1876, "until she lost her temper, Madame was a charming Frenchwoman. She loved dress and she had a genius in that way. She was exceedingly polite and her manners were very attractive. For all that, she was a cruel despot."

Much like an overbearing parent, Madame Talvande confused control with love, fully convinced that everything she did served the children's best interests. Her temper was fierce, and her severe tongue lashes reduced even the strongest and toughest girls to tears and shame. But for all her faults, Madame Talvande was proud of her school, proud of the building which her husband, Andrew Talvande, had bought in 1819. So why, then, did she choose to overdose on morphine in 1828? What caused her to take such desperate measures? Two names should suffice to answer the question: Maria Whaley and George Morris.

Maria Whaley first attended Madame Talvande's school as a 15-year-old, the beloved daughter of Colonel Joseph Whaley. As strict as Talvande was, she could not contain Maria's free spirit or control her desires. When Maria met and fell in love with a man from New Jersey, George Morris, the colonel implored Talvande to do all she could to keep the two apart. Maria was from South Carolina and her father was not about to allow her to marry a Yankee. In his mind, Yankees had no respect for Southern traditions and culture, and their views on the abolition of slavery threatened to divide the country even further. But George and Maria would not be kept apart. The more Talvande tried to tighten her grip, the more Maria slipped from her grasp. The colonel was furious when he discovered that Maria had accepted George's proposal of marriage.

Eyewitnesses have seen the spirit of the former headmistress walk through the iron bars of the Sword Gates.

As headmistress of a school with 100 students, Talvande found it all but impossible to keep a constant eye on Maria. The task became even more difficult when the school hosted a banquet and dance. Maria was allowed to enjoy the food and the company at the dance. Dressed in her best, Maria savored this sip of freedom and then promptly disappeared. She walked out of the building and into George's waiting carriage. Together they journeyed to St. Michael's Church where they were married. Maria returned only once to Talvande's school so she could gather her belongings and bid farewell to her former life.

Colonel Whaley was incensed; his influence was sizable in Charleston and he blamed Madame Talvande for his daughter's insubordination. Embarrassed, the headmistress erected walls that ran the perimeter of the school, their tops encrusted with shards of broken glass to prevent an escape like Maria's from happening again. Talvande struggled to protect her reputation, but the damage was done. After nine years of dedicated service to the daughters of Charleston, she saw that Maria's eloping could very well destroy her reputation and standing. She was right.

While Talvande could hardly be blamed for the actions of the girl, Maria's marriage to a Yankee was cause enough for scandal with the Southern gentility and it was Talvande, more often than not, who bore the brunt of its weight. Students were lost and Talvande grew weary of the stares and whispers that followed her everywhere. Everything that she had worked for was being lost. She procured morphine from a druggist, ingested it and settled in her bed to wait for death.

Talvande did leave an indelible signature on the house, which sits at 32 Legare Street. The prison-like walls around the school (now a private residence) still stand and have become somewhat of an attraction. The gates in the brick wall are known as the Sword Gates, and people have reported seeing a woman dressed in a 19th-century hoop skirt walk right through the wrought iron bars. She returns every evening at 9:00 and leaves two hours later. She sweeps through the house, walking through empty bedrooms to check upon empty beds. Old habits are hard to break, and it's no surprise that not even death can keep the dedicated Madame Talvande from checking up on her sleeping girls.

2
Slaves

Those Horrible Red Eyes
JACKSONVILLE, FLORIDA

Good and evil are often intertwined in the hearts of men. For the most part, individuals are able to resist their basest desires, and rarely do their acts reflect pure evil. But at Kingsley Plantation, a historic antebellum home in Jacksonville, Florida, evil still lives. The red eyes that tourists and residents have seen in their rearview mirrors when driving by the plantation late at night are the echoes of a slave who subjected three female slaves to torture, rape and murder. While slavery robbed a human being of his human rights, the murdered girls were robbed of their humanity.

The man for whom the Kingsley Plantation is named came to Florida in 1817 when he settled on Fort George Island across the St. Johns River from Mayport. His crops were Sea Island cotton, sugar cane, corn and citrus, grown for acres across the island and worked by slaves who were effectively trapped by the plantation's island locale. These workers lived in cabins that dotted the land, surviving as best they could. Slaves were permitted to work at a craft once their work for the master had been completed. The slaves were generously allowed to keep any profits they might have reaped from their work. Their freedom, however, remained a luxury they could not afford.

In 1806, Kingsley purchased a slave named Anna Madgigine Jai, when she was 13 years of age. Anna had just arrived from the chaos of religious warfare that was tearing its way through her homeland of Senegal. The two were never married legally, but that didn't prevent Kingsley from fathering five of Anna's children and proclaiming them all his legitimate heirs. Five years after Kingsley had obtained her as a slave, she was liberated to be his constant companion. For 23 years, the two managed Kingsley Plantation together. All the while, Kingsley continued to amass property and slaves; at its height, Kingsley's empire was composed of four major plantations, more than 32,000 acres and more than 200 slaves.

When the United States bought Florida from Spain in 1821, liberal Spanish policies were replaced with more restrictive ones. Interracial marriages were outlawed, and blacks, whether free or not, found their rights and freedoms limited. By 1837, Kingsley had had enough. Slavery, he believed, was a necessary evil in an agricultural economy. He perceived the changes in society's attitude towards his wife and children, and realized that only by leaving Fort George Island could their freedom be secured. They settled in the Dominican Republic, where their descendants live to this day. The plantation was sold to his nephew, Kingsley Beatty Gibbs.

As a historic site, the Kingsley Plantation provides invaluable insight into the underbelly of American imperialism. On Fort George Island tourists now walk where slaves once toiled. If it is their hope to connect with the past, then they could not do so more fully than at the Kingsley Plantation, where some visitors claim that the past is not just reenacted, but relived. When the Kingsleys left their plantation, they left behind a lasting reminder of one slave's evil.

The slave who raped and murdered three other female slaves could not keep these crimes hidden for long, and he found himself at the mercy of an enraged and unforgiving mob. He was beaten and his bloodied body was dragged down a narrow drive. A rope was cinched around the slave's neck and as the mob took their vengeance, the man's life slipped away. But when his blood was spilled upon the plantation ground, something else seeped into the earth too.

It's not known when the first sighting took place, but ever since that man's death, there have been rumors of a chilling sight. There is a one-lane road that runs near Kingsley Plantation. Surrounded on either side by woods, the road can, even on the sunniest and clearest days, still fall under shadow. At night, when the sky is dark and the land is still, the road becomes the setting for the slave's return from death.

In October 1993, a woman named Tes Rais, from Jacksonville, was driving along the road. It was dark, and Tes drove slowly, peering into the darkness that seemed to swallow up the light coming from her headlights. The road was deserted, but Rais periodically checked her rearview mirror. Each time she looked, she saw exactly the same thing: just the pitch black of the road behind her, rimmed on the edge by the red glow from her rear headlights.

She continued to drive along, singing to the Top 40 hits that blared out from her car stereo. And then, as she glanced in her rearview mirror, she was overcome with fear. She sped away down the road, certain that she would never forget the pair of red eyes that had appeared in her rearview mirror, two glowing red eyes that leered at her. If these eyes are indeed the legacy of the slave who raped and killed those young girls, it's not hard to imagine him stalking his victims with the same glower. The red eyes are impotent now, unable to carry out what surely must be the most sinister of intentions. For that, people visiting Kingsley Plantation are thankful; they are troubled enough with everything that the Kingsley Plantation represents: the subjugation of others and the evil of men.

Rotherwood Mansion
KINGSPORT, TENNESSEE

One historic mansion, two fantastic stories: one is a tragic tale of love lost, and the other an account of the ugliness of hatred.

The first story begins with the arrival of the Ross family in Kingsport, Tennessee, in the early 19th century. Reverend Frederick A. Ross and his family, wife Theodocia Vance and children David and Rowena, came to Kingsport so that the reverend could work as a minister in the Boatyard Presbyterian Church. Independently wealthy, the reverend ministered to the people of Kingsport for free. The family settled along Netherland Inn Road, where Ross built Rotherwood Mansion, naming it after the home of Cedric the Saxon in Sir Walter Scott's novel, *Ivanhoe*. Here, the Ross family prospered and grew. Little Rowena, with ringlets of brown hair and rosy, chubby cheeks, grew into a woman of charisma, beauty and grace. A grand pianist, Rowena Ross is believed to have been the first to play Beethoven in the state of Tennessee. After her education at the best schools in the North, Rowena returned to Sullivan County. Her transformation did not go unnoticed. Those who had known her as a child now marveled at her as a woman. To the chagrin of most other young women, men considered Rowena the fairest of all and many desired to make her their bride.

Unfortunately for these suitors, Rowena's heart already belonged to a boy from a neighboring town. What had started as simple infatuation grew into something deeper as the two exchanged letters over the years. When she accepted his proposal, the hopes of all the bachelors in town were dashed. As for the rest of Kingsport, Rowena's engagement was the source of great excitement. The Rosses were known far and wide, and as soon as people heard about the impending nuptials, they began making their way to Kingsport. The wedding promised to be the social event of the season. As the wedding approached, few recalled having ever seen Rowena so happy. But her joy was short-lived.

The day before the ceremony, Rowena's fiancé decided to take some of his friends fishing on the Holston River, which bordered Rotherwood. Rowena watched from the shore as her husband-to-be cast his line about, talking and joking with his friends. One second, her love was there, tall and strong in the light of the afternoon sun; the next, there was a cry, a splash and he was gone. Although bubbles rose and broke the surface, his body did not. It was later found floating downstream. The death plunged Rowena into a depression and for two years she remained cloistered within Rotherwood Mansion.

Eventually, she reappeared, wary and weary, but ready to begin living her life again. Her eyes had lost their glimmer and her stare was often vacant, but enough of Rowena's light remained to draw the attention of a wealthy young man from Knoxville. No one could replace her first true love, but Rowena was fond enough of the rich suitor and accepted his proposal of marriage. For the first time in years, Rowena allowed herself to believe that she might soon be happy again. Falling in love with Rowena, however, seemed to be a fatal omen. Her new fiancé fell ill and Rowena's worst fears were realized when it was evident he had contracted yellow fever. Within days, he was dead. Once again, Rowena plunged into depression, but this time she never recovered. She walked into the Holston River one evening and was dragged to its depths as the water caught hold of her heavy clothing. Some romantics believe she heard the voice of her first true love calling out to her from the depths of the river.

Rowena's death was only the beginning of the end for the Ross family. Reverend Ross missed his daughter and believed that he saw her walking the banks of the Holston River on moonlit lights, scanning the waters for any sign of her lover. Each time he saw her, however, he had to remind himself that she was dead and the reality of it was almost too much to bear. His work began to suffer, as did his finances. Ross' fortunes dwindled and he was forced to sell Rotherwood Mansion.

The buyer was Joshua Phipps, a universally despised figure in the town. Kingsport was known for its abolitionist leanings, and while there are some who claim that Phipps' legendary cruelty and hatred towards his slaves were exaggerated in order to bolster a cause, his slaves would likely differ. He beat them relentlessly through the night, filling the air with the sounds of leather lashes meeting and breaking skin and cries of anguish and pain. More than a few travelers dreaded passing by Rotherwood late in the evening where the screams of Phipps' slaves assaulted the senses. Phipps' slaves refused to suffer in silence. Invoking the spirits, the slaves placed a curse on their cruel master.

In July 1861, Joshua Phipps took ill. A fever overwhelmed him, sapping his strength and health. Phipps couldn't move from the bed where he lay, so he brought in a small slave boy to sit beside his bed, fanning him. But the curse was gaining momentum. As Phipps lay in bed, drifting in and out of consciousness, he heard a strange buzzing. Through eyes he could barely open, he saw a black cloud moving in through the open window. The small boy entrusted with fanning him sat at the foot of the bed with a look of contentment on his face. As the black cloud approached, Phipps realized he wasn't looking at one solid mass as he had first thought. The cloud was alive with the wings and buzzing of thousands of flies. Phipps was aghast, throwing up his arms as the cloud descended upon his ravaged body. They filled every orifice as the small boy watched, knowing that the invoked spirits were doing their work. Phipps was smothered to death. But, even the hand of death cannot still some evils. Phipps would return; his spirit would stand in sharp contrast to that of Rowena's.

Rowena, after all, has returned to Rotherwood out of love. She walks the banks of the Holston River, always with the hope that the one true love of her life will resurface from the Holston's watery depths. Hers is a solitary journey, her only companions pain and loss. And while she laments the untimely deaths that robbed her of her happiness, Phipps seems to revel in his fate.

The first signs of trouble came when Phipps' body was being transported up a hill for burial. Almost all of Kingsport had lined the road to catch a glimpse of his casket. As the horses pulling the hearse strained to climb the hill, people pulled their jackets tighter around them as a wind began to blow and dark clouds blocked out the warmth and light of the sun. More horses were hitched to the hearse, and as it began to move up the hill again, lightning arced across the sky and the ground shook with thunder. As the crowd huddled closer together and wondered if the weather was an omen, the coffin flew open and a large black dog leapt from the hearse and ran down the hill. No sooner had the dog disappeared from sight than the clouds opened, loosing a torrent of rain on Kingsport. The crowd dispersed, leaving only the gravediggers to rush Phipps' coffin into its grave.

Since that time, Phipps' spirit, which is said to manifest itself in both the black dog and as a mischievous apparition, continues to torment the living in Rotherwood. His eerie, high-pitched laugh has been known to echo through the mansion's halls, while those sleeping comfortably in their beds often wake to the sight of something tearing their blankets and bedsheets from their bodies. The black dog has been seen running across the grounds after storms. For years, a visit to Rotherwood has meant glimpsing the best and worst of humanity: Rowena's unrequited love and Phipps' insatiable hatred.

Things might have changed, though. Since 1991, Dr. Lenita Thibault has lived in Rotherwood Mansion. She has restored and upgraded most of the house and while aware of the mansion's haunted past, she claimed, in an interview with the *Kingsport Times News*, that "this is a warm and fuzzy house. It's warm and inviting and it talks to me in that respect." Phipps' spirit, which had always roused anxiety and unease, may have been quelled through the redemptive power of Rowena's quest to find everlasting love.

These Old Eyes
CHARLESTON, SOUTH CAROLINA

The former slave stood on the pier, listening to the water lap against the supports. The air was warm and thick, almost heavy. But as he stood there, bathed in the orange glow of the setting sun, mirrored on the ocean's rippling surface, he drew a breath, savoring its aromas and taste before exhaling. There was a time when the heat and humidity would have been oppressive, almost noxious. Now, it was glorious and divine, like the first warm soothing touch of his wife after a long day working in the fields. But that was in the past. No longer would he work under the stifling heat of the sun, picking rice for white-skinned masters who sat watching and luxuriating in the shade. He had earned his freedom, impressed the slave owners enough to convince them to grant him his humanity once again.

He had his freedom, but he still wondered what he would do with it. Slavery was all he had ever known and what lay before him now was uncertainty.

Doubt can cripple a man, and it crippled the ex-slave to the point of inaction. Doubt had turned into fear and the ex-slave took to watching the piers from St. Philip's Church cemetery for hours on end, wordless and still. As the days passed and the sun rose and set, the freed slave could feel time and his life slip away like grains of sand through his fingers. He tried to remember the feeling of elation and joy that had coursed through his body when he first learned that he was being freed.

But the feeling had faded long ago and as he sat in the cemetery surrounded with the voices of the dead, he wondered why he was so dismal, so despondent. When he thought about it, he realized that he felt alone, adrift and aimless. On the plantation, at least he knew where and how he belonged. But here, in the world of his former oppressors, he was no one. His apathy grew unchecked and soon he was mired in a deep depression, unable to eat. He could feel death's approach and he thought back to how he had arrived at this place. You could say it started with eyes.

• • •

When he was a slave, he had been known as Boney. His home could be found on King Street just behind Colonel Andrews' Colonel Towne Mansion. Of course, during the day, one rarely found Boney at his house. Every day, Boney, tall and lean, was at the wharves, unloading sacks of rice from the colonel's ships. It was tough, demanding work but he excelled at the labor. His strength never flagged and he always found the time to help those weaker than he. With a nod, wink and a grin, he'd continue to hoist the heavy burlap sacks while others sat down around him to catch their breaths.

Others regarded Boney with some suspicion. Despite his phenomenal strength, he was better known for his remarkable visual acuity. Where most people could only see a ship approaching on the horizon, little more than a silhouette, Boney could see the figures on the ship's deck, even capable of describing people's clothing. There were those who marveled at Boney's gift, while others, like most people when encountering something strange and foreign, treated the man as if he were cursed. Some took to avoiding the man with the "crazy eyes." Boney could sense the trepidation and the fear.

He retreated to Charleston at night, away from the prying eyes of his fellow slaves. In Charleston, he could lose himself in the crowds. He walked for hours through the city, often along the same path, and it wasn't long before he became a familiar sight to those who lived along his route. One of those people was a man named Peters. Peters was familiar with Boney in more ways than one.

Each seller had to have an agent, someone who could act as an intermediary between producer and the consumer. Colonel Andrews' was Peters. Peters knew Boney as a hard and able worker who worked for one of his favorite clients. Andrews' rice came with their husks already removed, meaning it was ready for immediate shipment and could be sold for a higher price. The higher price translated into increased profits for both agent and

seller. Every now and then, Peters joined Boney on the latter's late night walks and became quite fond of the slave.

He realized the tall, wiry slave was an intelligent and
well-spoken man who knew more about his owner's business that he first thought. Peters began wondering why
Boney never seemed to pursue his freedom, how he never
broached the topic. He described a slave named Caesar,
who had won his freedom when he came up with a con-
coction that many believed could draw the poison from
an adder's bite. When he registered the invention, his
owner was suitably impressed and freed Caesar.

One evening, while walking and talking, Boney looked
to the skies, his eyes growing wide with what he saw. He
turned to Peters and said, "The church is on fire." Peters
looked up to the black sky but saw nothing but the spire
of St. Philip's Church towering over the city. He saw
nothing else—no flames, no smoke.

Boney raced towards the church as fast as his long
spindly legs could carry him. He had to get there before
the whole of it was ignited. St. Philip's Church had stood
since 1710, one of Charleston's oldest Episcopalian
churches. Many of Charleston's finest attended service
there, including Peters and Colonel Andrews. When
Boney reached the church, he looked up to the steeple and
saw flames curling their way up the spire into smoke. He
set his jaw, grunted and began to climb the walls of the
church up to the spire, using gaps in the brick and mortar
exterior and outcroppings of mortar as his feet and hand
holds. He gritted his teeth, and his breath came out short
and ragged. Lifting sacks of rice was one thing; surmount-
ing the church was completely different. His muscles

stretched and pulled and cried out in pain. His fingers quivered, threatening to lose their already tenuous grip on the concrete, and his legs trembled.

But Boney refused to stop, and soon he stood atop the church, with the spire burning overhead. One shingle burned there; how strange, thought Boney, that the church had not yet gone up in flames. Still, he wasted no time in reaching for the shingle, tearing it away with his bare hands that burned in the fire. He cast it to the street below, where, deprived of fuel, the fire extinguished itself. The rest of the flames Boney put out with his shirt.

When he finally came back down to the street, it was to a crowd of people who had gathered to watch Boney save the church. Colonel Andrews was there and so was Peters. Peters could be heard describing how Boney's telescopic eyesight had picked out the fire long before any significant damage could be done, that Boney's eyes were a gift, not a curse. Boney was quiet, uncomfortable with everyone staring at him. He mumbled a thanks before escaping into the darkness.

When the sun rose over the wharves of Charleston the following morning, Boney was already at the docks, ready to greet the first of the colonel's ships and begin hauling the sacks of rice. But before he could, Peters approached him and told him that the colonel wanted a word with him.

Boney entered the colonel's office where his owner stood, smile on his face. He took Boney's hand, thanked him profusely for saving their house of worship the night before. Boney remained modest, saying he had only done what he had to do. The colonel wasn't finished yet though.

He told Boney that he was free, that his actions the night before had bought his freedom.

• • •

The days were long now, almost meaningless. That night that had completely changed Boney's life. He had craved freedom for so long but had despaired of ever acquiring it. He gave up hope long ago and now found that he was right to have done so. There was nothing for him here. He might have saved the church and been set free, but he still felt like a black man in a white man's world.

Boney died not long after and was buried in the cemetery at Colonel Andrews' Waccamaw River plantation. But he later returned to haunt the plantation on which he had spent a majority of his life. Tourists walking the grounds would often stop where they walked, whispering to one another that there was a strange black man resting against a tombstone. All he did was stare out into the distance, out towards the ocean with brilliant white eyes that burned themselves into the memories of those who saw them.

3
Mansions

A Word About Glass
COLUMBUS, MISSISSIPPI

Nellie Weaver sat on her porch, rocking back and forth ever so slowly in her rocking chair. The sun burned orange in the setting sky, and Nellie savored its fading warmth. Gazing out across the expanse of land that her father had acquired throughout his years, Nellie reflected upon her life and could only shake her head and smile with some regret at how her life had become so different from anything she imagined and hoped for as a child.

She had, of course, been born into privilege. Her father, William B. Weaver, had made his fortune in Columbus, Mississippi, as a merchant. To showcase his wealth and provide a house for his family, Weaver built a grand mansion just north of Columbus on the outskirts of the city in 1848. When completed, the Weaver mansion was considered by many to be one of the grandest and finest homes in the state. The elite of Columbus clamored for an invitation to grace its halls and dine beneath the opulent chandeliers. As soon as she was old enough, Nellie took over hosting the dinner parties and social functions for which her family was famous.

Nellie was the perfect hostess. Graceful, intelligent, charming and beautiful, Nellie disarmed even the most demanding guests with a radiant smile and a kind word. She loved entertaining, but while she was happy to meet and greet the guests, she was happiest when she was with Charles Tucker. Of all the men who came calling and who sought her company, none moved her or caught her eye

Nellie Weaver, the former mistress of Weaver House, announced herself to the new owners by etching her name into one of the windows.

quite like Charles Tucker. He was everything she had dreamed of as a child when she pictured her groom waiting with anticipation as she walked the aisle, her father's arm intertwined with hers. In Charles, she placed all her dreams for family, love and happiness. None of them would work without his presence.

In 1878, the couple was wed in a grand ceremony that few would ever forget. Nellie was a vision in white, and

the only thing that could exceed the brilliance of her diamond ring was her smile. To commemorate the day,
Nellie took her diamond ring and with it, carved her
name into the window of the south parlor. The Tuckers
spent a few years of wedded bliss in the Weaver mansion,
and whenever Nellie felt unsure of herself or was
unhappy, she would cast her gaze upon the south parlor
window and remember the ecstasy she had experienced
on that storied day.

Soon the Tuckers had another to share in their happiness. Nellie gave birth to a daughter, Ellen, and for a short
while it appeared as if she had everything she ever
wanted. But, as it is with so much in life, Nellie's happiness was fleeting at best. For whatever reason, Charles left
the Weaver mansion one morning and never returned,
abandoning Nellie and Ellen to their fates.

Nellie, though devastated, had been raised to perse-
vere. She opened a private school to support herself and
her daughter, but the money earned from the venture was
not nearly enough to maintain both the splendor of the
house and well-being of her family. The mansion fell into
disrepair, and Nellie took to spending more and more
time rocking back and forth in her chair. Whenever
pedestrians walked by her perch, she would ask them to
stop for a while, for she had stories to tell and they had
ears to listen. She regaled listeners with accounts of the
Weaver mansion's past glory, of the people who had once
passed its threshold and how it pained her that the house
should be reduced to such a state. It was a Weaver legacy
after all, and while it had become the source of great
heartache (Nellie found it nearly impossible to look at her

name etched into the glass of the south parlor window), she still loved the house and wanted those in Columbus to remember its glory and who had been responsible for its construction.

Nellie Weaver died in her 80s during the 1930s. Her death, like her marriage, was tragic. She died from burns that she received when her dress caught fire, ignited by sparks from a fireplace in the rear parlor. By the time of her death, the Weaver mansion was in danger of succumbing to years of neglect. Few could believe that the run-down home was once considered the finest of its kind in the state. Indeed, few alive then could even recall the days when the Weaver mansion served as the setting for dinners and parties with exclusive guest lists. For years after Nellie's death, the house sat, squalid and ugly, abandoned and falling evermore into disrepair.

But one woman, Mrs. Erroldine Hay Bateman, saw something majestic and palatial in the ruins. In 1950, she bought the property and set about restoring the house. Her heart ached when she first saw Nellie's name etched into the south parlor, knowing that it represented the loss of innocence. She knew how Nellie had spent the final years of her life; restoring the home was perhaps Mrs. Bateman's way of restoring some of Nellie Weaver's dignity in the only way she knew how. But one item would remain untouched. According to Kathryn Windham, author of *13 Mississippi Ghosts and Jeffrey*, Mrs. Bateman said, "We must save that pane. It will be a touching reminder of Miss Nellie and her life in this house."

Of course, no sooner had the decree been issued to the workmen than one of them carelessly swung the end of a ladder through the window that Mrs. Bateman had placed under protection. The name was lost forever. Mrs. Bateman was disappointed but knew that accidents would happen and could not deny the fact that the mansion, which she now called Errolton, was becoming as beautiful as she had imagined when she first glimpsed its sagging walls.

In the mid-1950s, restorations were complete and the Bateman family moved into the mansion, eager to make their mark in the house's history. They had no way of knowing that the next chapter in Errolton's story would be written by none other than Nellie Weaver.

Lying on a sofa that she had recently purchased for the south parlor, Mrs. Bateman found her comfort soon disturbed by the bright sunlight streaming through the windows. She got up and went over to the windows where she began pulling down shades and then stopped. Bending down, Mrs. Bateman ran her fingers along one of the windowpanes. It looked as if there were dirt or grit there. She peered more closely and drew a breath in shock. It wasn't dirt that was marring her window; a name had been scratched into the pane. Mrs. Bateman realized that this pane was the one that had replaced Nellie's. There, etched on the glass from the inside, were the letters N, E, L, L, I and E. No one in the house took responsibility for the signature. Mrs. Bateman thought it might have been a guest from one of their dinner parties, but she had cleaned the windows just the day before. The etching had happened overnight.

Mrs. Bateman attributed the etching to the return of Nellie Weaver to Errolton. Nellie had always loved the house and agonized over her inability to maintain its luxury in her fading years as money became scarce and her strength failed. The mansion's restoration had restored something of Nellie as well, and Mrs. Bateman believed that the etching meant that Nellie Weaver was pleased and satisfied with Errolton.

White Oaks
CHARLOTTE, NORTH CAROLINA

Known by many names, it is the greatest of the colonial mansions that grew out of the Myers Park neighborhood in Charlotte, North Carolina. It has 52 rooms, two wings and acres of landscaped grounds complete with fountains. It is known primarily as the only house James Buchanan Duke ever owned in the state with which he is almost synonymous. Duke also owned homes in New York City and New Jersey and used the Charlotte mansion as a temporary residence when he was in the city on business and as a means of introducing his young daughter to the customs and values of the South. He assembled 12 parcels of property, creating a holding that exceeded 15 acres and expanded the original existing house. That house today bears his name, but it is also known as Lynwood and White Oaks. The house was granted National Historic Landmark status on the basis of its association with Duke, a noted philanthropist and tobacco king. The property, however, also become known for its other owners, among them, Jon Avery.

When looking for a house in Charlotte, Avery stopped in at the Duke mansion and was taken with its splendor and craftsmanship. He lingered on the brick terrace lined with lush gardens of dogwoods and azaleas and marveled at the manicured lawns and marble fountains. Avery knew the mansion was perfect for his family. While the initial days spent in the mansion were full of joy, the euphoria didn't last. Avery's wife was suffering a mental illness, and the family could no longer deny that she required confinement in an institution. With great reluctance, Avery accepted his physician's recommendation and had his wife committed. Avery spent as much time as he could with his wife, but as the days passed, she became less and less herself. She spent most of his visits just staring blankly at something beyond her room. He eventually gave up.

Then someone else came into his life. A reporter for a local paper came to White Oaks to write about the mansion's storied history. The chemistry between Avery and the writer was palpable and although she was aware of his wife's condition, she found herself accepting his dinner invitation. As the pair began spending more time together, it was no longer possible to deny that Avery's intentions went far beyond friendship. Hers did too, but she knew that they could never weather the scandal if he should decide to leave his ailing wife for another woman. Tragedy was all that she could see before her and she made the painful decision to stop her relationship with Avery. Avery was heartbroken, but he knew that she was right. Before they parted, he asked of her one favor: to meet him a year later, regardless of circumstance, whether they be dead or alive, at ten minutes to midnight in the circular garden near the fountains and brick terrace. She agreed.

A year later, they met as planned. Even in the pale blue glow of the moonlight, the woman was as beautiful as ever and Avery's chest heaved with the beating of his heart. But much had changed over the year, and the bloom on their love's rose had faded. Her heart already belonged to another but Avery was still able to wrangle another promise from her to meet him again at ten to midnight a year later.

But many things change with the passage of time. The reporter had become engaged and she did not arrive at the appointed spot and time alone. She came with a roommate, feeling it inappropriate to meet Avery by herself. Ten to midnight came and went and still the reporter waited. Then, like a whisper, she heard his steps soft upon the wind, light and almost ethereal. She turned and there he was, walking across the terrace; he looked tired and weary. He was a shadow, dressed in dark clothing, a wraith in the moonlight. Perhaps he suspected the truth of what the reporter had to tell him. He approached her, drawing ever closer. She opened her arms wide, ready to accept his embrace, but was shocked when he walked right through her. Although no words passed across his lips, she heard his voice clearly in her head saying, "Dead or alive."

It's not every day that someone passes through your own solid flesh and bone. Feeling a need to investigate further, the reporter discovered that Jon Avery had died weeks earlier. She wept when she learned that while he lay on his deathbed, he used his last breath of air to ask, "Dead or alive? Will I make it?" Even as he marched towards death, he thought not of his mortality, but of the reporter who had charmed his heart and to whom he had made a promise.

So while his body lay rotting in a cemetery, his spirit carried on, determined to touch Venus one last time before he began eternity in the afterlife. When the reporter, out of curiosity, returned to the mansion again another year later at ten to midnight, she heard Avery's footsteps light upon the cobblestone walk. Again, he passed through her body as if she were ethereal, only this time, as he faded into the night, she heard him whisper, "Goodbye." After that, the writer never did return to White Oaks, and Avery's ghost was never seen again. It's comforting to think that he has found his peace in the afterlife after one last glimpse at the woman who allowed him to experience, one last time, the sensations of unfettered and transcendental love.

Mordecai Manor
RALEIGH, NORTH CAROLINA

Raleigh, North Carolina, owes its existence to Joel Lane, owner of one of the largest plantations in Wake County in the late 18th century. In its day, the plantation produced a variety of goods from produce to medicinal herbs. The Lane family lived in a house that Joel had built for his son, Henry, in 1785. It was a glorious home and became the social hub for the local communities. When city planners were trying to decide where to begin building their capital city of Raleigh, commissioners originally wanted to buy land across the Neuse River from Colonel John Hinton but were swayed in favor of Lane when the latter invited the committee to his home for food and drink the night before the vote. For £1378, the committee acquired 1000 acres of land, and the city of Raleigh was born.

Despite Lane's prominence in Raleigh's origins, the neighborhood that grew out of his plantation does not bear his name. Instead, a visit to North Carolina's capital and Lane's former plantation uncovers a suburb named Mordecai, a neighborhood known as the birthplace of Andrew Johnson and as the continued home to Margaret Lane, granddaughter of Joel. It is Margaret's ghost now who serves as a reminder of Raleigh's origins.

When Joel Lane died, ownership of the house transferred to his son, Henry, and his family. Their daughter, Margaret, married Moses Mordecai, a lawyer and judge. Together, they had three children and enjoyed their position as part of Raleigh's social elite. But an illness claimed Margaret's life when she was still very young.

Mordecai remarried, choosing to remain entrenched in the Lane family by marrying Margaret's sister, Ann. She bore him one child before Mordecai succumbed to an illness in 1824. His will provided for an expansion of the house, which was completed two years later. But even though the house had lost its patriarch, the plantation was able to survive and even prosper, as five generations of Mordecais lived, worked and died there. So large was the plantation that even after the Civil War had dulled its prominence and prosperity, three separate neighborhoods were able to claim land from the plantation. But lest anyone forget the contributions of the Lane family, the spirit of Margaret Lane remains to remind any and all individuals of their place in Raleigh's history.

The city of Raleigh bought the house in 1967, along with its furnishings, in order to preserve and honor the Mordecai legacy. Also restored along with the home were a number of other structures from the plantation, including a stonehouse, a kitchen and a garden. Other historical buildings from around Raleigh were relocated here, including a post office from 1847, a law office from 1810 and a church from 1840. Taken together, they formed Mordecai Historic Park, a living museum in more ways than one.

The centerpiece of this historic district is, of course, the Mordecai Manor, a two-story mansion open to the visiting public. The house is decorated with 18th- and 19th-century furnishings, creating the most authentic experience possible. It is cared for and looked over by guides and a cleaning staff who roam through the house every night, sweeping out and wiping up the day's dust.

One hot afternoon, a housekeeper, forehead glistening with sweat, worked cleaning the dining room. The house was closed to the public at the time, and there was no reason to hurry. She could be slow and deliberate, enjoying the peace and quiet. With the dining room clean, the housekeeper moved into the hallway and began to wipe down the woodwork that adorned the dining room entrance.

As she worked, someone caught her attention. One of the manor's guides appeared to walk out of the library, which struck the housekeeper as odd. Hadn't all the guides already gone home for the day? Wasn't she supposed to be alone in the house? The guide was dressed oddly, not quite in step with the fashion of the day, in a long, black pleated skirt, a white blouse and a black tie. But she looked somewhat familiar and the housekeeper had no reason to suspect that it wasn't anyone other than a guide who had stayed behind to do some work.

The housekeeper saw the guide approach and turned from the woodwork to say hello. The guide, however, walked by the housekeeper, not even acknowledging her presence. There was a confidence and an assurance about the guide's stride, a bearing that suggested that she was not of the same rank as a lowly housekeeper. Her curiosity piqued, the housekeeper watched as the guide walked into the parlor. Dropping her towel into a bucket, the housekeeper walked in after the guide, determined to find out why she had been snubbed in such a manner. But there was one small problem. The parlor was empty.

The housekeeper stopped in the room's entrance, looking from one end to the other. Except for the curtains rustling in the breeze, everything was still and quiet. The guide couldn't have just disappeared from the parlor; the housekeeper was standing in its only entrance and exit. And then, she remembered. The woman she had known in the pleated black skirt was no employee of Mordecai Manor. The only reason she recognized the woman was because she bore a striking resemblance to the portrait she gazed upon every day when she cleaned the parlor. The housekeeper was sure she had seen the resurrected spirit of Margaret Lane Mordecai, first wife of Moses Mordecai and arguably the first lady of Mordecai Manor.

Mrs. Mordecai may not have been the first woman to live in the historical landmark, but she was the first to live in it under the name by which it is now known. In life, her authority in the household was complete. She was stern but never harsh, and while there was little that could rival her affection for her husband and children, her love of Mordecai Manor came close. It's where she spent the happiest years of her brief life. Her return, of course, is hardly a surprise. An untimely death combined with a fondness for the house has brought Margaret Lane Mordecai back to her house where she walks its floorboards, ever watchful, making sure that Mordecai Manor is being well taken care of.

Orna Villa
OXFORD, GEORGIA

Dr. Alexander Means was a distinguished man in many fields. Teacher, artist, inventor, minister and scientist: Means was all of these. Were it not for a rare instance of short-sightedness, Means would be the name forever associated with the invention of the light bulb.

Means' curiosity was piqued after a trip to the laboratory of Sir Michael Faraday in Great Britain. Means began conducting his own experiments with electricity and after perfecting his method, offered a demonstration at Atlanta's old city hall on June 2, 1857. Rotating a large disk through a machine, Means was able to create frictional electricity that he passed through wires into black carbon. The charge caused the carbon to burst into light. One witness at the demonstration claimed, "Never…have

I seen a more brilliant light. Nothing in all the phenomena of our wonderful age has ever impressed me more than this exhibition and I can never forget it as long as my memory lasts." But Means never realized the commercial possibilities of his invention and left the patenting of electric light to Thomas Edison. When Means first demonstrated his machine, Edison was all but 10 years of age.

Instead, Means is remembered as both an educator and a statesman, having served as a member of the 1861 Georgia Secession Convention. Of course, mention the name Means in Atlanta today and one is as likely to conjure up paranormal associations as those scientific or political, because Means left behind quite the legacy when he passed away June 5, 1903.

Originally from North Carolina, Means bought his Atlanta home in 1825. Its distance from the city allowed him to enjoy both the urban and rural aspects of life. Named Orna Villa, the two-story Greek revival home was originally a one-room log cabin built in the 18th century. Means adapted the house for his own uses, transforming a second-floor bedroom into a laboratory. Late into the night he worked in the lab, alternately amusing and frightening passersby with flashes of a brilliant green light that illuminated the night sky.

For years, people stopped to stare up at the second-floor windows of Orna Villa. They continued to do so even after Means' death, as the experiments continued well into the evening. New owners of Orna Villa were perplexed, puzzled as to mysteries of the phenomenon. The home's many residents also heard the footsteps of a person who was never seen, only heard. And while the source of the green lights was never in question, debate still rages over what spirit is responsible for the pacing heard outside on the rear porch.

The two most likely ghosts are Olin and Tobe Means. Olin represented everything that Means hoped his children would be, while Tobe, the youngest child, was the opposite. One night, Tobe and his father quarreled over the young man's future. Instead of going to college right away, Tobe wanted to travel around the world. The two argued through the night, but Tobe would not be convinced. He eventually stormed out of the house, never to return. And while there were times that he longed to return, he never got past the porch. He would walk up the steps, the wooden planks creaking and groaning beneath his feet. But he never got farther than the door. His hand would rest on the brass doorknob before he would turn and go off into the night again. The first couple of times it happened, Means rushed to open the door but found himself staring at nothing.

Conversely, Olin Means loved to study and became a doctor. But he also had a deep longing to serve God and the conflict plagued him day and night. Olin and his father talked long and often about the dilemma, talks during which Olin paced the back porch again and again. Before he could make a decision, however, Olin was stricken with an illness that medical science could not cure. God, it seemed, would settle the issue for Olin.

The first to report detailed accounts of the hauntings at Orna Villa was E.H. "Buddy" Rheberg in 1945. Rheberg's father-in-law had been, in his youth, one of Tobe's closest friends. So when Rheberg bought the house he was quite aware of its paranormal past. Still, when the inexplicable happened, he was taken by surprise. One winter morning, Rheberg had just sat down to breakfast when he heard steps on his porch. He assumed it was Walt, his handyman, and he yelled at Walt to come in, that the door was unlocked. Walt never entered. Instead, the footsteps started up again, went to one end of the porch and then came back to the door. Rheberg stood up from his meal in frustration, walked to the door and flung it open. The porch was empty. Rheberg walked out, looked around and saw nothing. Walt showed up half an hour later, assuring Rheberg that he had only just arrived.

Rheberg's wife described how the house was never silent, how the quiet was always punctuated with squeaks and creaks. She'd thought it was just the floorboards warped with age, until the fateful day she decided to paint the kitchen floor. The whole time she was painting, she couldn't shake the feeling that there was someone in the room with her, watching her as she painted. When she finished, she picked up her supplies and locked the door to the kitchen, to keep forgetful family members from treading in it. She needn't have worried, though, as she was alone in the house.

Yet when she later unlocked the kitchen door to examine her handiwork, she was unsure how to interpret the single footprint that had appeared in the center of the room. There were no tracks leading into the kitchen and none led out. There was just the single footprint. Had Olin or Tobe returned to see what the Rhebergs were doing to their family house? Not long after, groceries began disappearing from the Rhebergs' refrigerator. Fresh biscuits went missing, joining milk and cake on a list of items that were pilfered regularly.

The Rhebergs' daughter, Betty, was terrified when she heard someone coming up the stairs one night. Her parents had already gone to sleep. Her voice quivering, Betty called out into the darkness, asking if it was her father approaching. There was no reply, just the creaking of footsteps that got louder as they approached the landing. She watched in a mixture of fear and amazement as the door to her bedroom opened; when she realized what was happening, she screamed.

Rheberg rushed to his daughter's bedroom, where Betty demanded to know if her father had seen the figure who had opened her door. Rheberg shook his head, capable only of offering his assurances that they were indeed alone in the house.

The Rhebergs soon began to attribute all strange events in their house to the presence of a spirit. Researching the history of the Means family and the folklore of the house, they were quite certain that the apparition responsible for the haunting was Tobe Means. "There's Tobe again" became a familiar refrain in the Rheberg household.

In 1967, the Wattersons bought Orna Villa, and their time there was punctuated with unexplained acts of mischief. The new family could not as easily bear the ghost's presence; they didn't care who the spirit was, they just knew that their home had come under siege. Whatever spirit it was that haunted Orna Villa, he or she didn't seem to take to the Wattersons. As is often the case, an unwelcome renovation may have upset the paranormal entity.

The porch that Tobe and Olin used to pace was turned into a den. One night, James Watterson was sitting in his rocker, watching the magnificent view afforded by the large windows he had installed. He saw the flicker of a shadow pass in front of his eyes. Startled, he turned towards the hallway behind him that led to the kitchen on the left and the parlor on the right. The kitchen door was open, as always. The parlor door was always kept closed, but before his eyes, James saw the door open. Alone in the house, Watterson felt fear and panic at what he had just witnessed. He left the den and walked the house, turning on lights in every room. But all the search confirmed was his solitude.

It was just the beginning. Watterson had converted one of the rooms into a display area for his collection of Civil War antiques. The assorted uniforms, muskets, swords and regimental flags were all placed in display cases. The muskets were placed on wall-mounted brackets above a long, glass display case. James and his wife were startled one evening when a loud crash came from the room. They rushed to the room where they saw eight muskets lying on the showcase. The brackets on which they had rested looked as if they had been pulled from the wall. Most perplexing of all was that the antique glass display case was not damaged in the slightest when the eight muskets came crashing down upon its surface. The glass bore not even a scratch.

Not long after, Watterson was dusting and polishing items in his Civil War collection when he stopped to admire the six valuable lithographs that he had hung on a wall. Suddenly, all six lithographs fell from the wall and crashed to the ground. Watterson rushed over to see if the images had been damaged in any way and was relieved to realize that they had sustained no damage. But then he wondered why none of the frames were damaged. Why wasn't any of the glass in the frames cracked? And how did they all fall at the same time? When he examined the backs of the frames, Watterson discovered that the wires stretched across their backs had come loose.

In 1975, a doctor bought the house, and it seemed that the resident spirit became restless. The doctor's family saw again and again a tall, thin figure in a long coat walking their hallways. The apparition resisted all attempts at communication, stopping during his walks occasionally to play with the doctor's daughter's toys. But the doctor, like Olin Means, was pious, and he prayed that the spirit leave his home if it were anything but a protective entity. If it were a guardian angel, then it should, at the very least, stop frightening his family. The good doctor's prayers appeared to have been answered. The disturbances dropped off and the family could almost believe that their house had always been normal. For seven years they lived in the house, free of any sort of interference until one night in 1984 when two Methodist ministers stopped to stay at the house.

The guests slept in the room adjoining the old porch where Watterson had watched the parlor door open on its own. Before retiring for the evening, they had asked their hosts to wake them up at eight in the morning and not earlier. The hosts were a little surprised to find their guests sitting at the breakfast table drinking coffee when they came down to wake them up. The hosts learned that the ministers had woken at six in the morning when someone or something had pounded on their door. The spirit of Orna Villa, it seemed, had been awakened.

But who exactly is haunting Orna Villa? Most theories center on Tobe and Olin, though some argue that Tobe lived a long and happy life in Arkansas and feel it is unlikely that he would have any reason to return to Orna. One family member, a niece of Olin's, always felt that it was her uncle who haunted the house, and she said as much in a book called *The Ghost of Orna Villa*.

Regardless of who the ghost is, Means, the scientist in the second-floor bedroom, must have work to do. If it is Tobe who has returned in the afterlife, Means might be seeking to heal their fractured relationship. If it is Olin pacing the porch, Means will no doubt lend a ready ear and a steady shoulder again for his son.

Barnsley Gardens
SAVANNAH, GEORGIA

"I wouldn't do that if I were you. I reckon you'd be having a mighty unfortunate streak of bad luck if you did."

Godfrey Barnsley sighed. He'd been hearing the same thing, sometimes with better grammar, but always with the same dire warning against building a house upon the hill in Cass County. People kept mentioning something about an old Cherokee Indian curse and how bad things would happen to anyone who lived on the hill.

"The land is sacred," an old Cherokee man had told him. "Touch it and you and all your family will suffer."

Barnsley would not be swayed. He didn't believe in luck, good or bad. The ideas of ordering principles, of ideas like fate or destiny, were nothing more than a society's desires to place order and the rational upon completely random events. Barnsley believed in the individual, in forging a destiny all your own. His own life stood as testament to that belief.

Barnsley had first emigrated to America when he was 18, destitute, with only four shillings in his pocket. Within a decade he had transcended his humble origins and, through hard work, discipline and dedication, acquired a sizable fortune in the cotton trade. All this success he had achieved in just 10 years, and while there had been lean times, Barnsley was certain of himself and never saw failure as even a remote possibility.

Helping to ease the initial troubles was a girl, the daughter of a prosperous shipping merchant named

William Scarborough. Her name was Julia, and Barnsley approached wooing her with the same single-minded and focused dedication with which he approached his work. The two were wed on Christmas Eve, 1828. Six years later, the couple was one of the most beloved and respected in Savannah.

Little wonder, then, that Barnsley stared at the old Cherokee man with more than a shade of skepticism coloring his complexion. His life had told him that nothing happened that wasn't part of his own design. And while he respected the wizened Cherokee man and could see, hear and feel the weight of the wisdom that sparkled in his eyes, Barnsley just said, "I don't believe in superstition. I never have. If I want to build my home up on the hill, that's where it's going to go."

"So be it," said the old man. "I have warned you." The old man walked away, and though he tried to deny it and blamed it on the chill air, Barnsley felt a shiver run through his body as he watched the man shuffle away. There was dread in the air, but Barnsley ignored it, waving away the slight apprehension he was feeling with a quick wave of his hand.

The land was perfect for a new home. He and Julia, with their burgeoning family, needed the space to look after and to care for their children. He had first seen the hills of northwest Georgia when traveling to Lookout Mountain on a wagon train and was immediately taken with its tranquility and bucolic splendor. It helped that two of his closest friends endorsed the location. The Reverend Charles Wallace Howard and William Henry Stiles both had bought land in Cass County and insisted that Barnsley join them in their idyll. The decision was made easier when Barnsley's family doctors told him that his wife's tuberculosis was worsening and that a move to the mountains, where the air was crisp and clean, might benefit her. Barnsley was desperate to help Julia. Her coughing fits were becoming more frequent and she was getting weaker; he trembled whenever he found blood in her handkerchief. Barnsley bought 10,000 acres of hills covered in thick woods surrounding a spring.

The landscape inspired Barnsley to name the property Woodlands. As an amateur architect of some note, Barnsley began drawing up plans for the mansion. Drawing upon the styles of Andrew Jackson Downing and Calvert Vaux, Barnsley imagined a grand Italianate manor bordered with elaborate gardens—a rock one with a statuary and an Oriental one with a fish pond, a deer park and a bog garden with a multitude of aquatic plants. Recalling the trees he had seen in catalogs, Barnsley ordered cedars from Lebanon, lindens from Germany and sequoias from California. As for the house, tied to nature at is was, it would be modern in every sense of the word with 14 bedrooms, flushing toilets, hot and cold running water and a gigantic stove on which cooks could prepare feasts fit for royalty.

So that Julia would understand what he was envisioning, Barnsley drew up elaborate sketches and diagrams that gave her great comfort. At the time, they were living in a log house that was damp and drafty in the winter, conditions that exacerbated her coughs to the point where her entire body would be racked with pain. Construction on the hill was slow and labored as the hilltop was flattened shovel by shovel. The soil was used to make bricks with which Barnsley planned to build his home.

Barnsley was discouraged, though. Every morning, as he rose out of bed to check on Julia, he could see how much of her life had ebbed away. Slowly but surely, his wife was dying. She was but a wisp of her former self, and in 1845, with construction on the mansion still years away from being completed, she had no choice but to return to Savannah and her doctor's care. There, she died.

With her death, Barnsley lost the will to continue. He stared at the drawings tacked up all over the log house, remembering the many talks Julia and their wonderful children had had regarding the placement and design of certain elements. Furiously, he tore the drawings down. To look at them was to be reminded of her touch, her voice, her breath. Casting his eyes skyward, he whispered, "What would you have me do?"

He didn't receive an answer that satisfied him, so Barnsley threw himself into his work. It was the one thing remaining to him that he had begun before Julia had entered his life.

But as it happened, Barnsley chanced upon a séance while he was in Mobile on business, and it was there that he discovered himself once again. The medium promised him that he could, through the practice of spiritualism, speak with his dead wife again. That night, in a dusty little room at the back of a dingy inn, Barnsley sat in a candlelit circle and attempted to contact his dead wife. While he was initially skeptical, Barnsley's depression had led him to consider methods he might have once deemed superstitious to help him grieve.

Barnsley returned to Woodlands a new man. His children couldn't help wondering what was behind the sudden transformation. Their father had left for Mobile a sullen, distracted and irritated man; upon his return, he acted as if he had been reborn, dipped in magic waters that renewed his spirit.

"How was the trip?" they asked him.

Barnsley just smiled and said that he would be going for a walk among the boxwoods on the property. "Oh, and one last thing," he said as he turned to go outside. "We start construction of the home as soon as possible. It is what your mother would have wanted."

The children smiled, still in some disbelief that their father had returned to them the way he'd once been. The children, of course, couldn't understand what had happened. But then, one day, they noticed Barnsley walking the grounds outside the house under the trees, mouth moving as if he were speaking to someone or something who wasn't there.

He blushed slightly when his children asked about it and said, "You want to know with whom I've been speaking? Let me tell you. I've been speaking with your mother. She has returned; she is here. She walks the land, not alive, but not yet dead. She does send her best, children. We will spare no expense in the construction of this mansion."

Over the next decade and a half, artisans and workmen toiled at Barnsley's vision. He imported the finest materials that he could find, tiles from Stoke on Trent, doors and paneling from London and marble from Italy and France. Completed, the manor was as stunning and opulent as any in the state of Georgia.

But as blessed as Barnsley might have felt, to the outside observer, there was surely some truth to the old Cherokee man's words. After all, Julia had died after construction began on the hill and not long after her death, an infant son of theirs passed away. A year after the home's completion, daughter Adelaide died in the house. Barnsley's eldest child, Howard, was murdered in 1862 when he encountered a band of Chinese pirates as he searched Asia for plants that might be transplanted to Woodlands. By that time, of course, Barnsley had matters that demanded his immediate attention. The suspected curse had fallen upon the house itself.

The Civil War was upon Georgia, and as a slave owner, Barnsley was considered a threat. Barnsley's friend Colonel Robert G. Earle of the Second Alabama Light Cavalry rode out to Woodlands in the spring of 1864 to warn of the advancing Union troops. Barnsley watched in horror as Union troops gunned the Confederate colonel down from behind. Barnsley buried the body behind his house. Fortunately for Barnsley, he treated black and white equally, with a respect that impressed Union General McPherson. McPherson left standing orders that the mansion was not to be touched. Yet as soon as he rode from Woodlands, scavengers and stragglers flooded in, pillaging the property.

The conclusion of the Civil War ended years of bloody warfare, but its affirmation of Union governance and everything that came with it—the abolition of slavery and the fall of the Confederate government—meant the end of Barnsley's wealth and prosperity.

"All is lost, my daughters," he said as the Barnsleys reunited at Woodlands. "My ships are gone and so is the cotton." He sighed and peered out across the hazy landscape, still smoky with the fires that burned all over Georgia and many of the Southern states. "This is indeed a cursed land. It has taken everything of mine."

Barnsley was determined to restore the splendor of Woodlands and moved to New Orleans to see if he could to do just that through the restoration of his cotton business. Success, which had come to Barnsley easily in his youth, was now elusive. He died in 1873 in New Orleans, leaving the New World in the same way that he had entered it: almost penniless.

His dogged determination had passed onto his daughter, Julia. She and her Confederate captain husband, Baltzelle, returned to Woodlands after living in Savannah, and Julia was ever hopeful that she could do for Woodlands what her father could not. Her brothers had fled to Brazil, where it was said that ex-Confederates would be greeted with open arms and where they could leave the curse of Woodlands behind.

Julia, however, felt it her duty to restore the manor. After all, she was her mother's namesake. Who had more right? With her husband and daughter Adelaide, named for her dead aunt, Julia set about repairing the damage vandals from the war had done while they had searched the mansion for gold. Her husband turned his attention to making money for his small family.

Woodlands may have been robbed of almost all its wealth, but as Baltzelle stood in the manor's tower surveying the land below him, he realized that the woods were still wealthy with natural resources. The lands, the thousands of acres covered in trees, were rich with lumber that could be cut down and shipped all across the smoldering South and used in its reconstruction. His eyes twinkled when he realized that the seeds for Woodlands' resurgence lay within the woods.

Alas, Baltzelle couldn't escape the power of the Cherokee curse. Julia's husband was crushed when he was loading logs onto a train. The logs shifted and rolled from their perch onto an unsuspecting Baltzelle. With news of his death, Julia had had enough. She gathered her things, took Adelaide in her arms and left for New Orleans to join her ailing father. There she stayed for over 10 years, returning once to Woodlands when her father died in 1873 and his body was returned for burial. She returned for good 12 years later, in 1885, when her husband, a German sea captain named Charles von Schwartz, passed away, leaving her with no income of her own and with nowhere to go but Woodlands and its majestic ruins, memories and tragedies.

Despite all that had happened on the property, when Julia saw it again for the first time, she couldn't hold back the tears that fell from her eyes. They were borne out of loss and of nostalgia; in her mind's eye, Julia struggled to remove the vegetation and weeds and vines that looked as if they were choking the home and land.

As Adelaide walked around the manor, she heard and saw all sorts of things that she couldn't quite explain. When she walked under the boxwood, she always saw a woman walking ahead of her, whose resemblance to her grandmother, Julia, was more than just passing. Adelaide was convinced that her grandfather was right, that he had had many conversations with his dead wife long after her death.

Adelaide smiled when she realized that her grandfather had returned to Woodlands to be reunited with his wife. Not only was he buried there, but every day, just before suppertime, a chair could be heard scraping across the floor in the balcony. It's said that the noise, in life, had signaled the time for Barnsley's pre-dinner cocktail. And in the corridors, Adelaide heard the laughter of children, her dead aunts and uncles at play.

As Adelaide grew, so did her obsession with the restoration of Woodlands. She married a man who shared her passion, but the two never had the funds necessary to begin the renovation project. When he died, Adelaide's dream of returning Woodlands to its prime died too. She was left with two sons to rear. So Adelaide began breeding in her sons the desire and the will to do what she could not. Adelaide would have been wise to heed the advice that her grandfather had ignored. Even when a tornado tore the roof off the house in 1906, Adelaide stayed.

There was something about the land that was beyond their comprehension, and the Barnsleys continued to hold to their beliefs about their immunity from superstitions. Adelaide's insistence that her children, Preston and Harry, dedicate themselves to the home's majesty only ensured that they would be the next victims of a curse that had begun three generations before.

Preston and Harry, while devoted to their mother, were quite different with each other. All that existed between them was enmity and suspicion, fueled by highly competitive drives. Preston took his energy into the boxing ring, while Harry enlisted in the army and fought in the trenches of the First World War. Preston, however, was a less-than-adequate boxer and was forced to retire early when the many punches to his head resulted in severe damage to his brain. His personality was significantly altered, and his time in the ring left him a little different. While his friends attempted to have him committed, Adelaide believed that all Preston needed to recover was to stay a little while at Woodlands where the surroundings were familiar and where he could be close to his mother's love. It was a decision she would come to regret.

One evening, while she was discussing the grounds with Harry, Preston walked into the room. He was drenched with sweat. His eyes were wild and crazy, black holes from which no humanity spilled. Adelaide stood up with a start. "Preston," she said, "are you all right? You don't look well."

"Oh, I'm perfect, Mum. Better than ever," he said, stepping forward in time with the monotonous cadence of his voice. "You see," he continued, "I've figured it all out. It's been Harry all along. He tried to have me committed all so he could get Woodlands for himself. Don't you see? He's after it all. But I'm too smart. I'm too fast. I've beat you, Harry. I win."

Preston pulled a gun from his pocket and shot his brother in the heart. The retort echoed through the air and then there was silence. And then the wails of a mother, watching her son die while cradling his head in her arms.

Preston closed his eyes and collapsed to the floor, a small smile on his face. He was committed to a state institution, leaving Adelaide alone in Woodlands, where she continued to hear the ghosts of her long-dead relatives, testaments to the curse. She nodded, for now she believed.

After her death, it seemed as if the succeeding generations were all too wary of the house's past. They sold off bits and pieces of the land until fewer than 1200 acres of the original 10,000 remained. The home was left untouched and fell deeper and deeper into ruin. It seemed that Woodlands would wither and fade away into nothingness.

But in 1989 a German prince, Hubertus Fugger Babbenhousen, bought the site, determined to transform the magnificent grounds into a succession of gardens, the Barnsley Gardens. Wary of its suspect past, the prince listened to the locals and recruited two Cherokee chiefs to come to the land and remove the curse. They did, and today the Barnsley Gardens is a luxury resort set amid the verdant splendor of the bucolic paradise Godfrey Barnsley had loved so much. Over 150 types of roses now thrive in these gardens and where people once feared to tread, they now do so, awed with the spectacle of nature's beauty.

It's said that Godfrey and Julia walk the gardens hand in hand, relieved at last that they are together, living the afterlife within the dream landscapes of their lives.

4
Plantations

Living Ruins
COURTLAND, ALABAMA

Between Town Creek and the Tri-Cities of Alabama, there is a field. To the unobservant eye, little in this field distinguishes it from any other. It is windswept and tangled with bleached underbrush. But there is more here. Reluctantly, faintly, the land can be coaxed into giving up its secrets. Vegetation bends and dips, teasing out small hints and reminders that there was once a footpath. A closer look reveals more. Bricks lie tangled among the weeds, the baked earth cracked and weary with age. Proceed further and the underbrush gives way to packed earth that vegetation is just beginning to reclaim. There is a pattern here, the outline of something grand and magnificent. It is the footprint of what was once a glorious plantation home in Courtland, Alabama.

Known as the Rocky Hill Castle, the home was built in the late 1840s and early 1850s when James Edmonds Saunders decided to settle there so he could grow cotton. Business was steady and Saunders prospered; his wealth was mirrored in the grand estate he built for himself, a grand two-story mansion with porticos, Doric columns, a cupola and custom-made furniture. Yet it was not enough for Saunders. Seeking to augment his wealth, he had tunnels beginning in his basement carved out to the banks of the Tennessee River. From there, slaves were taken from the barges and ships that traveled the Tennessee and sent to work Saunders' fields. Given Saunders' prominence and place in Alabama society, it's no surprise that when the

Civil War threatened Alabama soil, Saunders would take up arms in the name of the South.

Saunders first acquired a reputation for himself when he moved to Courtland from Virginia. He was a lawyer by trade and his practice in Courtland was successful, allowing him access to the upper stratospheres of society. His connections served him well when he began to entertain his dreams of owning a plantation. He was able to amass hundreds of acres in a short period of time and become one of the leading cotton producers in northern Alabama. If the North were to claim victory in the Civil War, he would stand to lose substantially. He rose quickly through the ranks of the Confederate army and became a colonel. His home became the setting for many meetings involving high ranking Confederate officials, including J.L.M. Curry and General Pierre Beauregard.

During the war, Courtland never did come under Union control. But slavery had been abolished and with its fall, Saunders' plantation and all his wealth were lost. He tried his hand at a number of other ventures but with no success. Vineyards withered, with grapes dying on the vines. Acres and acres were lost in order to pay for debts that accumulated far too quickly. But Saunders persevered, and was able to keep possession of his greatest prize, his home. For years, the house was passed down through the hands of Saunders' descendants. One, Thomas Saunders, discovered that the house was much more than it appeared.

Try as she might, Thomas Saunders' wife never could get comfortable living in the mansion. It wasn't that she didn't like the home. On the contrary, she loved it when she first walked through its halls. The place was stunning, still decorated with furniture that James Saunders had built specifically for his home. She luxuriated in the green velvet love seats, the marble-topped tables and the oil paintings in their gold-leaf frames. But as the days passed and she became more and more acquainted with the house, she began to feel as if there were something strange about the place. She couldn't quite define it, but she could feel a growing sense of unease and discomfort permeate her soul.

It began with the growing feeling that she was always being watched. She felt as if someone were boring into her with their eyes, but whenever she looked around her, she saw nothing. She was always alone. Even when she started hearing things in her basement, she was always alone. Was she going crazy? Why was she constantly hearing the clanking of chains from the basement or tappings on the walls of certain rooms? At a loss for what to do, Mrs. Saunders finally deferred to the house, demanding that whoever was causing the disturbances reveal him or herself or leave her in peace. The house fell silent and Mrs. Saunders allowed herself a self-congratulatory smile. The smile faded when a voice from the house's depths rose up from the silence. According to Michael Norman and Beth Scott, the hushed voice said to Mrs. Saunders, "Do not be doubting for I am truly here."

But who was there? Mrs. Saunders did not know until that day. She was coming down the steps of the home's magnificent spiral staircase and saw, at the foot of the steps, a woman in a hoop skirt. The fashion wasn't contemporary but Mrs. Saunders thought nothing of it. It was Courtland's centennial and many people were going around in costumes in preparation for the celebrations. The home had been receiving visitors for weeks now, drawing those interested in their community's past to the architectural gem to learn more about the past. Mrs. Saunders greeted the visitor with the same wide welcoming grin with which she favored all visitors. She introduced herself and then offered the woman in the dress her hand. The strange woman didn't take it; instead, she chose to fade away and disappear into nothingness, leaving Mrs. Saunders in shock. Thomas and his wife were among the last of the Saunders to call the Rock Hill Castle home. It's not known if the house's resident spirits had anything to do with decisions to sell the home to two Courtland businessmen in 1926, but the move was the beginning of the end for the mansion as a family home.

Tenants moved in and out of the house, always whispering about a shadow that moved across the land and building. The phenomenon was relatively innocuous but still disturbing enough to the tenants that their stays were both brief and memorable.

In addition to the woman in the hoop skirt who continued to appear at the bottom of the staircase, there was talk concerning another spirit, a woman who walked the path from Rocky Hill Castle to a nearby creek. This apparition appeared to the unsuspecting dressed in gray, her face the portrait of eternal grief. She walks the path from the house to the creek and back again, wandering the path she took the day the bridge over the creek collapsed.

The rain had been hammering for days at the shingles of Rocky Hill Castle, the house where the woman and her two children lived in a rented room. When they drew back the curtain one morning to reveal the sun-dappled acres surrounding the mansion, they knew that they could finally go outside again. They decided to have a picnic down by the creek. They walked down the path that led to the little wooden bridge that crossed the creek. The creek, swollen with rainfall, had spilled over its banks and rushed furiously along its path. Tentatively, mother and children began crossing the bridge, but its supports were old and weathered, woefully inadequate to resist the force of the raging creek. There was an audible crack and then another as the support beams split apart, collapsing the bridge under the family's feet. They plunged headlong into the torrent, the children swallowed up underneath the froth and foam. The mother fought as best she could, but her water-soaked clothes were like lead and she was dragged beneath the surface.

Years after the deaths of the mother and her children, people out for walks along the path to the creek would return home shaken and disturbed, discomfited by the visions they had seen while walking. The reports were dismissed at their onset until the disbelievers saw for themselves what had frightened so many others before them: the dripping, gray-clothed woman whose eyes were full of sorrow and grief. Witnesses of the water-logged apparition reported feeling overwhelmed with misery and loss after seeing her. She quickly became as much a fixture of Rocky Hill Castle as the mansion and its assorted spirits.

By the late 1940s, however, the castle was far removed from its position as the seat of power for the once-mighty Saunders dynasty. The home had fallen prey to vandals who made off with the home's furniture collection, while those looking for access to easy wealth pried up floorboards and bore through walls in search of hidden treasures. The walls became graffiti murals.

Even after Rocky Hill Castle had succumbed to the ravages of time and collapsed to the ground in a heap, the ghosts lingered, unwilling to relinquish their homestead. The house clung to its past, and late at night, it's been said that passersby could hear a piano being played from within its abandoned walls. The field is home now to the spirits of Rocky Hill Castle, and they are the lasting reminder of the glory and prominence that was the Saunders plantation of Courtland, Alabama.

Art Lives
CHARLES CITY, VIRGINIA

When Martha Pratt left the New World to study in the Old, all she left behind was an unsigned portrait of herself that hung on the second floor of the grand Shirley Plantation in Virginia. Pratt had intended to return to North America, but when she met Hugh Griffith and fell in love with the dashing Englishman, she married him and lived out the rest of her days in England. But while she never returned to Shirley Plantation, subsequent generations of her family continued to work and live at the plantation. They began to wonder whether Martha Pratt had ever really left.

The oldest plantation in Virginia, Shirley Plantation has stood since 1613, just six years after Jamestown was established as the first permanent English colony in the

New World. It has been in the Hill family since 1660, when it was granted to Edward Hill, and is the oldest family-owned business in the U.S. The mansion, which has spawned so many stories for which it is known today, was begun in 1723 by Edward Hill III for his daughter Elizabeth and her husband, John Carter. Martha was Elizabeth's aunt. The house was completed in 1738 and quickly became the social center for prominent Virginian families such as the Harrisons, Byrds, Lees, Washingtons and Tylers. Its famous flying staircase, which rises three stories with no visible means of support, is the only one of its kind in North America.

In addition to its social prominence, this National Historic Landmark has played a political role too. It once served as a supply center for the Continental Army during the American Revolution, was the birthplace of Ann Hill Carter, mother of Confederate General Robert E. Lee, and survived the Peninsula and Petersburg Campaigns of the Civil War, the conflict in which Lee rose to national fame. The plantation that sits on the James River is still home to the 10th and 11th generations of the Hill-Carter family that first occupied Shirley Plantation in 1723.

But Shirley Plantation's oddest and most peculiar chapter began in 1858, years after Martha Pratt had passed, leaving behind just a portrait to remind those of her place in Shirley Plantation's history. That year, her descendants decided to move the portrait from a second-floor bedroom, where it had hung for over a century, to a mantel in a third-story bedroom. But the move breathed life into an energy that had lain dormant for years. As they paused to admire the painting in its new place of honor, the family heard a gentle knocking. They couldn't determine where it was coming from; it was almost imperceptible, but slowly it increased in volume and intensity. The sound was coming from the painting, from the rattling of the frame against the wall. As if moved by unseen hands, the painting was shaking back and forth. The family stood in the bedroom, flabbergasted at the sight taking place before them.

The noise became so persistent that the family moved the portrait to the attic, hoping that whatever forces were rocking the portrait against the wall would stop. But in the attic, the rocking of the picture only intensified, and it rattled and clattered its way across the floor like a dog unleashed. Unsure of what to do next, the Hills moved the portrait to the main floor, and for a while it seemed as if they had calmed the restless spirit. Within weeks, however, the first floor was filled with the sound of the painting pounding against the wall. Finally, it was put in what was once Martha's second-floor bedroom, where the painting fell silent, and so it stayed there for over a century.

By 1974, the painting had been quiet for years, though many still recalled the mystery and intrigue of the famous portrait. When the Rockefeller Center asked for paranormal items for an exhibit, the Virginia Travel Council lent Martha Pratt's portrait for the occasion. The portrait was taken off the wall on the second floor of Shirley Plantation and sent to New York City. The painting arrived at Rockefeller Center without incident, but that changed once the portrait had been placed inside a display window.

Visitors to the exhibit watched with amazement as the painting swayed back and forth so vigorously that objects around it began to rock as well. Employees would return to the center in the morning to find the painting lying on the floor, having somehow broken free from the display case. A reporter working for NBC had recorded the swaying phenomenon on tape. At a loss as to what to do, exhibitors decided to place the piece in a storage room, but, as it was in the Shirley Plantation, the move did little to quell the restless painting. From inside the storage room came knocking and crying sounds that only grew more persistent as time passed. Employees found it difficult to concentrate on their work as their offices became soundboards for the cacophony. When the painting of Martha Pratt was returned to Virginia, the Rockefeller Center celebrated a quiet return to normalcy.

As for the painting, the frame was in desperate need of repair. Those who speculated that Pratt's spirit was unhappy to be in New York City and wanted to return home might have been correct. The painting was sent to the Linden Galleries in Richmond, Virginia, for repairs, and craftsmen wondered if the portrait was trying to break free of its frame. But while New York City had experienced agonizing wails and cries, Richmond had a far gentler experience. Pratt's spirit seemed much more at ease with the comforts and gentility of the South than of the North.

While it was at Linden Galleries, employees noted that the painting did behave oddly, but rather than shake, it vibrated, and instead of crying out in anguish, it emitted a sound not unlike the gentle tinkling of bells. The stories the people of Richmond had heard were true; after all, there were no bells inside Linden Galleries. Martha Pratt must have acquired some for her stay.

No one knows what happened to Martha Pratt after she married Hugh Griffith in England, but one thing her painting made clear was that it's always good to go home. The portrait was eventually returned to Shirley Plantation where it was again placed in its old second-floor bedroom. Today, Martha Pratt continues to smile down upon her descendants.

Waverley Mansion
COLUMBUS, MISSISSIPPI

To look upon Waverley Mansion today is to see the history of Columbus, Mississippi. It is a grand mansion, a study in opulence rendered in four stories and white-painted pine. Yet just 50 years ago, the home had been decrepit. Vegetation had invaded; the floors were buried beneath years of detritus, hidden underneath a thick mat of leaves, branches, garbage and other waste. Vagrants slept there, looking for shelter from the elements. Everything changed when Robert and Donna Snow found Waverley. The Snows restored the mansion to its original glory. But during its renovations, strange things began happening, occurrences that could only be attributed, in the end, to the presence of spirits from Waverley's colorful past.

Columbus first rose to prominence as most cities in the South did: through the production of cotton and various other crops grown on vast plantations that ran for acres and were worked by slaves. In the years leading up to the Civil War, the city thrived. And one of those attracted

Waverley Mansion in Columbus, Mississippi

to its promise of wealth in return for a little hard labor was George Hampton Young, a colonel from Georgia. In 1852, he began construction of his home along a gentle knoll that sat near the Tombigbee River. Six years later, through the design of architect Charles Pond and

work of artisan Richard Miller, the mansion was completed. Its crowning touch were English boxwoods that
Mrs. Young, who died before the home's completion, had
planted at the entrance. The plants are still there today.

Over the years, Young's prosperity was such that his
plantation soon resembled a small village. With over 1000
laborers, it was easy to understand why he needed to con-
struct a post office, a brick kiln, a cotton gin, an ice house,
a lumber mill and a leather tannery. For his family, he built
massive gardens and marble-lined swimming pools that
dotted the 40 acres upon which his plantation sat.
Waverley became the social center of Columbus, with
weekly dances held in its grand ballroom. Things changed,
however, when the newly formed Confederate States of
America opened fire upon Fort Sumter in North Carolina.

Although federal troops never occupied Columbus, the
city did find the transition from an economy with slaves to
one without devastating. Waverley was no different.
George Hampton Young died in the home in 1888, and
successive generations of Young children lived there until
Captain William Young, the youngest child, died there in
1913. Waverley then sat abandoned for years, its 40 acres
slowly reclaimed by encroaching forest and wilderness,
until the Snows arrived and began their work. The home
today is listed as a National Historic Landmark.

But was the home ever completely abandoned? Ghosts
had been seen in and around the house since the last
Young passed away. There is the mythical figure of Major
John Pytchlyn, who died in 1835 after living an orphaned
life under the care of the Choctaw Indians. It's said that he
loved riding his horse near the Tombigbee River, often

passing through Young's plantation on his sojourns. The phantom riding begins with the faint sound of pounding hooves in the distance. They get louder and louder until the earth is shuddering and you feel you might get trampled. And then there he goes—brushing by but causing no stir in the air. The hoofbeats fade and you're left wondering whether what you just experienced actually happened or was a figment of an overactive imagination. Colonel George Hampton Young, still a man of impeccable Southern charm, has also been known to appear in mirrors throughout the house.

The Snows found themselves asking many questions when they heard a little girl calling out for her mother. Mrs. Snow first heard the voice two years after she had moved into the mansion. She was sitting in an armchair reading when, from somewhere outside, she heard a plaintive voice crying, "Mama! Mama!" Mrs. Snow put her book down and walked to the open balcony door. She peered out over its edge, ready to greet one of her own children, but she saw nothing but the manicured lawn. When she asked her children about it later, none of them could recall having been outside, calling for their mother. Mrs. Snow might have thought one of her children was playing a prank on her, but over the years she continued to hear the voice every afternoon. The same plaintive voice no longer startled her but it did concern her. She wondered what could have upset the child so much. Of course, it was a mystery that would never give up any answers.

After five years, the ghost became more assertive. She began following Mrs. Snow about the house, calling out to

On many occasions, owners of the house have heard the ominous cries of an unidentified little girl.

her from different parts of the home. Far from unwelcome, the pitter-patter of the ghostly feet became a soothing accompaniment to Mrs. Snow's days. And then, at night, every once in a while, Mrs. Snow would wake from sleep, roused from slumber by her children. They would ask her if the ghostly little girl was all right, because they could hear her crying through the house. Mrs. Snow hoped that she was. She hoped that the little girl was comfortable and thought she must be when she'd spot the indentation of a small figure seemingly asleep in a four-poster bed.

But then one day Mrs. Snow was preparing dinner when she felt someone brush up against her. She turned, but no one was there, and then, from out of the silence, came the voice. "Mama! Mama!" the girl cried, more desperate and distressed than ever before. Mrs. Snow was concerned, but all she could do was ask the girl what was wrong. That was the last the Snows heard from the girl for years. While she was absent from their lives, the Snows attempted to discover who the little girl might be, but found few answers.

Ten years later, Mrs. Snow was walking by the four-poster bed so favored by the little girl when she noticed that something was lying on it. She had made the bed carefully that morning, and now she saw an indentation in it. The little girl was back.

Even now, the little girl still makes an occasional appearance in the Waverley Mansion. Many have caught a glimpse of the little spirit walking the halls in her nightgown, tresses of dark blonde hair cascading over her shoulders. Her identity remains a mystery, but she is as much a part of Waverley now as George Hampton Young, tied indelibly to Columbus and its past.

Bonaventure
SAVANNAH, GEORGIA

Josiah Tattnall, Jr., sat and watched his house burn. With silver knife and fork in hand, he cut another piece of turkey on his plate. He speared the meat with his fork, then paused and looked at the guests all around him, their faces bathed in the orange glow of the raging fires that were now consuming his home. They stared at him, puzzled and a little frightened.

Just moments before, they had been sitting inside the house known as Bonaventure, congratulating his wife on the food and the beauty of the home. Their appetites had been stimulated with a combination of oysters and wine, and they sat with snifters of brandy as they waited for the presentation of the turkey. It was Thanksgiving, after all, and what would the day be without turkey? But just then, amid the conversations punctuated with gay laughter and the tinkling of glasses, the butler had approached Tattnall, leaned in and whispered something into their host's ear. Tattnall had frowned for a moment before the grimace passed like a ripple. He stood up and wiped his mouth with a silk damask napkin.

"If you'll excuse me," he said. "There is a matter requiring my immediate attention. I will return shortly." With a nod of his head, Tattnall turned on his heel and followed his butler into the house.

His wife had looked upon her husband with some concern. It was unusual for him to leave the table when there were so many guests to look after; the guests shared her apprehension, but Mrs. Tattnall disarmed them with a small smile.

"Oh please continue. Josiah won't be but a minute. Please, have some more wine or brandy."

Tattnall returned just minutes later.

"My apologies to everyone, but there will be a slight delay in the serving of the turkey. We must first move the table and chairs outside and while the servants will help with this task, I would greatly appreciate your assistance as well." He sighed, but his voice remained calm, almost impassive. "This house will soon be engulfed with fire and there is nothing that we can do to extinguish the flames. However, the party will go on. Once outside and away from danger, we will serve the turkey. Now, please. Hurry."

Mrs. Tattnall rushed to her husband's side, and with a tremulous whisper said, "Josiah. Our home. What are we to do?"

Tattnall brought his finger to his nose, asking for quiet. "We will lead our dinner party into the garden, where we will dine under the stars and under the canopy of the oak trees that my grandfather planted so many years ago for my parents. We will eat from a menu of your design, drink the wine of the scuppernong grapes that have climbed our arbors for generations and bask in the warmth of our guests' company. And then," Tattnall said as he cast an eye around the dining hall in which so much of his life had been passed, "we will toast our health and say goodbye to Bonaventure."

Mrs. Tattnall buried her head in her husband's shoulder, trying to stop the flow of tears that had welled up in her eyes.

"No tears, dearest," Tattnall whispered to his wife, his mouth upon her ear.

"Apologies, my love. I was the one who insisted so upon lighting fires in the parlors."

"No apologies. Their light was warm, their warmth a comfort."

"Our world's on fire, Josiah."

"Yes, it is," he murmured. "To our guests, my dear. We must attend to our guests."

The massive table was lifted upon the shoulders of a small army of servants and the burlier of the dinner guests. Down the steps they went, where the table was placed upon the great stone terrace. So careful and steady were they that not even the fullest of glasses lost a drop.

A servant followed closely, bearing candles and lamps. Tattnall approached him.

"We've no need for candlelight or lamplight. Please, take them back inside. We dine by firelight."

The guests sat warily at their chairs, unsure of whether they should continue eating. But Tattnall took his seat at the head of the table and with a smile as warm and inviting as candlelight, begged everyone to enjoy themselves.

"We are the last guests of Bonaventure," he said. "Let us not be its dowdiest but instead, its rowdiest." He beamed as he saluted his guests and drank wine from the crystal flute in his hand. "We will drink and eat under this glorious canopy of oak until the sun does rise."

And so they did. Under the sky and the firelight, they ate their fill of everything that Mrs. Tattnall had cooked and prepared for days, ably assisted by her cooks. Bottles of wine were opened and consumed as servants did their best to rescue the vintages from the flames.

And when the first rays of the sun stretched across the land, capturing in their light the wisps of smoke that were all that remained of the grand plantation home, Tattnall raised another glass and made one last toast.

"To everyone gathered here for this night, we thank you for your company. Bonaventure will remember you. Always. May the joy of this occasion never end." Tattnall turned and cast his flute against the trunk of an oak tree. The stands of oak trees echoed with the sound of cracking glass and all present knew it was a salute to the grand home. They didn't realize how prophetic Tattnall's toast would be.

• • •

Bonaventure, meaning "good fortune," had been built years before to celebrate the union of two of the most politically and socially prominent families of colonial America. Yet while their children came together in blessed union, the fires of the American Revolution threatened to tear it all apart.

The Mulryne and Tattnall families had risen to power together in Charleston, South Carolina. Their shared experiences as they struggled with and then succeeded at their plantations forged a bond. It was a bond shared by their children, who grew up together almost as if they were brothers and sisters. When the Mulrynes moved to Savannah, Georgia, they took with them their daughter, Mary. It was a move that Mary silently opposed; she had grown up in Charleston and it was the only home she had ever known. And while as a little girl she had found her playmate, Josiah Tattnall, Jr., annoying, she was older now and had found that as they both gingerly entered puberty, they began exploring together the first faint stirrings of emotions that could only be satisfied with a tender touch or a warm embrace. But as much as she longed to remain in Charleston near Josiah, Jr., Mary knew, as a devoted and loyal child, that her place was with her family. As she neared Savannah, she clutched close to her heart the last words Josiah, Jr., had uttered to her.

"I will see you soon," he'd whispered into her ear. "That much I promise you, Mary."

The Mulrynes settled on land that became Bonaventure. They erected a grand mansion, built with brick imported from England. The landscape was carefully constructed and when Josiah, Jr., came west to ask for Mary's hand in marriage, Mr. Mulryne had planted, in secret, hundreds of oak trees. His plan was for the trees to grow thick and strong, forming an intertwined M and T as they did so. It would be a lasting symbol of the union between the Mulryne and Tattnall families.

The Mulryne and Tattnall families were joined in 1760 to great celebration and when Mr. Mulryne was finally able to steal a quiet moment with his daughter amid the hordes of well-wishers and guests, he presented her with his wedding present: the oak trees and Bonaventure. She was overwhelmed.

And so it was that Mary and her husband came to live at Bonaventure in wedded bliss, blessed with a joy that only grew and intensified with time, growing, just as her father had predicted, as the oak trees. Now grand and regal, the trees formed a sweeping canopy under which

Mary and her husband took countless walks, listening to the wind whistle through the trees and the Wilmington River gurgle and bubble as it rushed by the land.

They were blessed with two sons—John and Josiah III. Mary often took her children with her beneath the shade to tell them stories about their grandparents, about the deep abiding love that existed between the Mulrynes and Tattnalls and the planting of the oak trees. It was a wondrous place and the children loved spending their days playing on the grounds, learning to love the land and the state of Georgia.

When the first shots of the American Revolution were fired at Lexington and Concord, the once-prominent Mulrynes and Tattnalls found themselves standing outside of the society that had revered and honored them for so long. The colonies were clamoring for independence and loyalists such as the Mulrynes and Tattnalls were few in number. For a while, the families were able to avoid public prosecution for their loyalty to King George III because of their close ties to colonial governor James Wright. But when Wright was arrested and sentenced to house arrest on January 18, 1776, under the promise not to communicate with the British ships anchored just outside in the harbor, he fled his home under cover of darkness, fearful of the Patriots. Their militancy was particularly frightening.

He sought refuge at Bonaventure, where the Mulrynes helped him flee to Nova Scotia to await the outcome of the revolt. The Mulrynes fled to Nassau in the Bahamas, leaving behind their daughter and her family to take care of Bonaventure.

Times were difficult. Despite the presence of a Patriot government, the Tattnalls refused to tone down their vocal support for the British crown. While one must admire their integrity, discretion might have been better. Their neighbors, people who had once clamored for the Tattnalls' favors and attention, now cast accusing sidelong glances at them, shunning their company and whispering darkly about the family in suspicious voices. They could no longer walk about Savannah without hearing some sort of threat uttered in their direction. Finally, Josiah, Jr., and Mary had had enough. As much as it pained him to do so, Josiah, Jr., began making plans to take his family to England.

Mary looked at the horizon but saw only ocean. The only country she had ever known was changing, and it seemed that it would do it without her. It cleaved her heart to think that she was abandoning her wedding present to the Patriots; she prayed that if and when she returned, she could do so to the house that she could only now visit in the corridors of her memory. She prayed that the oak trees would remain unspoiled, that they wouldn't have to be cut down for timber and ruining forever what had taken her father almost a lifetime to create.

Six years later, Josiah Tattnall, Jr., returned to Georgia and joined with forces under the command of General Nathaniel Greene. The young Tattnall was pleased to write later to his mother that while the Patriots had occupied Bonaventure, they had returned it to him when they realized that he fought for their cause. The oak trees were more splendid than he remembered and he could only hope that he did them justice in his description to his mother.

He fought well in the war, and when America had finally secured its independence from Britain, he returned to Bonaventure with his wife. He dedicated his life to service in the name of the Republic, serving first as brigadier-general in the First Brigade of the Georgia Militia and then in the Georgia Legislature.

He thought often of his father in England and when he saw Bonaventure fall, he felt pain and agony. He had betrayed his father when he returned to fight for the revolutionaries, and now the legacy he had inherited was gone, consigned to the past. Two generations of Tattnalls had lived at Bonaventure; that would be all. When he toasted his guests and asked that the joy of the occasion continue forever, he hoped, within his heart, that those in Savannah would not forget the families who planted the Bonaventure oaks and the families who walked beneath them. While their politics had been different, father and son did love Bonaventure, and it was under the oaks where they both could find inner peace.

Josiah, Jr., loved Bonaventure and indicated that when he died he wanted to be buried in the shaded oak grove. His wife was interred with him later, as were his four children, none of whom lived past eight years.

In 1850, the last Tattnall to own the property, Josiah Tattnall III, sold 600 acres of the property to a prominent Savannah businessman, Peter Wiltberger. He opened up 70 acres of the 600 as a public burial ground, creating the Evergreen Cemetery of Bonaventure. Since then, it has become the final resting place of a number of Georgians, including Johnny Mercer and Conrad Aiken, and gained further fame when it was featured on the cover of John

Berendt's *Midnight in the Garden of Good and Evil*. It will, however, always be known as the home of the Tattnalls.

When Wiltberger purchased the property, it was under the condition that he maintain the family burial site. In time, the state of Georgia recognized the family by naming a street and a county in their honor. Tattnall's toast had come true.

Indeed, there are some who believe that to walk through Bonaventure Cemetery is to interrupt an everlasting dinner party. For among the stands of oak trees with their gnarled and moss-covered limbs, the Tattnalls are still entertaining their guests. Bonaventure has chosen to remember their joy forever. When the night air is calm and the sky is clear, the silence is broken with the clatter of dishes, raucous conversation and then there it is: the cracking of one glass followed by a host of others. It is Josiah Tattnall, renewing the toast he made so many years ago when he watched Bonaventure burn from beneath the canopy built as a monument to love.

5
Southern Women

Tinker, Tinker
GREENSBORO, ALABAMA

When Susian Truman Tinker passed away in Greensboro, Alabama, the cultural and social elite of the city mourned her death. During her given time on earth, Tinker had become a beloved and respected Southern belle. Polished, mannered and sophisticated, Tinker did her best to enhance life at a time when the strength of the Union seemed to be growing more and more perilous every day.

The question of slavery and its abolition was foremost on most people's minds. Secession had been carried through the legislatures of South Carolina and Virginia and it seemed as if the furor would soon envelop the genteel life of Greensboro. For Tinker, many hours were spent escaping the attendant pressures of daily political life in the beautiful home that had been built for her in 1835. Greensboro's guiding lights clamored for invitations to her banquets, as if being in her sphere was to absorb her radiance and humor. So when news of her death made its way through Greensboro, there were those who wondered what they would do now that she was gone. But for those who moved into her home, now christened the Tinker Place, there was little doubt that Susian Tinker hadn't allowed even death to keep her from continuing to live in the house that she loved so much.

A family with the name of Turpin came to live in the house, and Mrs. Turpin was the first to see the return of Tinker's spirit. Her family was sleeping when Mrs. Turpin woke them to tell them what she had seen. They gathered in the kitchen, and as they sat bathed in the warm glow of the kitchen with cups of warm milk in their hands, they listened as Mrs. Turpin described what she had seen standing in the parlor doorway.

Mrs. Turpin had crept downstairs, unable to sleep, book in hand. She planned to curl up in the old armchair by the window with a blanket. But when she got to the door of the parlor, someone was standing in her way, a woman dressed in gray, with a pleasant smile. Mrs. Turpin, far from startled, was filled with a sense of calm and warmth. The woman was obviously cordial and well mannered, a true Southern belle. And there was no mistaking the identity of the woman. Her face was identical to the one Mrs. Turpin had seen so many times in a sepia-toned portrait of the woman who had first owned the house. Mrs. Turpin was staring into the eyes of none other than Susian Tinker. The Southern belle faded from view, and the last thing to disappear was Tinker's smile.

While Mrs. Turpin was the first person to ever see Miss Tinker, she was certainly not the last. In 1934, Mrs. Turpin's daughter, Mrs. Waller, had her family and grandchildren over for dinner. The adults turned abruptly from their conversations to give their attention to the grandchildren, who had all dropped their forks onto their plates with a clatter and let out a collective gasp.

"Who's that?" they uttered with wide-eyed amazement. A lady in gray stood just a few feet from the table. She walked through the kitchen doorway, through the living room and then up the staircase where she passed into shadow. The children watched, eyes twinkling and colored with awe. The adults could only sit and stare; some of them had stopped eating their soup in mid-action, spoons frozen somewhere between bowl and mouth. Mrs. Waller smiled, recalling with fondness the night her mother had roused her from sleep to tell her about Miss Tinker's ghost. "That was Miss Tinker," she answered, and then began to describe how Miss Tinker was just a part of the house, just like the antique furnishings and the antebellum architecture.

One time, a sick friend was recuperating from her illness in an upstairs bedroom at the Tinker Place. Weak and dizzy, she found sleep elusive. Maybe a little reading would help. But the overhead light switch was on the opposite wall, and in her weakened state she was in no shape to walk across the floor to turn on the light. Mrs. Waller had placed a bell on the nightstand so the woman could call for anything she might need. The sickly woman rang the bell and called out, asking for light.

Mrs. Waller, sitting in the parlor, heard the chimes of the bell and began walking up the stairs to the bedroom. She found her friend sitting up in bed, staring at the light switch, perhaps wondering if she were sicker than she originally thought. After all, no sooner had the friend asked for light than unseen hands had turned the light on. Was she sick enough to be hallucinating? Mrs. Waller laughed, explaining to her confused friend how the long-dead Miss Tinker had a habit of returning now and again to help out around the house.

And then there was the first time Mrs. Waller encountered Miss Tinker in much the same manner as her mother had before her. She had woken on an ordinary morning and headed downstairs to start breakfast. Her slippers slapped against her heels as she made her way to the kitchen. At the kitchen door, she stopped. Standing in the doorway was a woman dressed in gray. She smiled, nodding towards the coming dawn, wordlessly wishing Mrs. Waller a good morning before she turned around and disappeared up the steps. Mrs. Waller watched her walk up the stairs, shook her head and then turned back into the kitchen to begin preparing the coffee.

Miss Tinker doesn't stay only in doorways, however. She can be seen warming her hands by a fire or walking in front of a cabinet, hands behind her back as she examines the crystal and china within. Attempts to talk with her have always resulted in her disappearance. Still, as a true Southern dame, she will not leave without first offering a smile.

The Love of Evelyn Byrd
RICHMOND, VIRGINIA

"Do you hear me, Evelyn?" William Byrd II slammed his fist down on his mahogany desk. "You will not marry this man. I forbid it. You will not fall in with that—that superstitious lot." He spat out the last two words, as if they had been laced with poison. He walked over to his beautiful daughter and put his arm around her shoulder.

"Evelyn," he said, the anger fading from his voice, "please listen to me. Who have you trusted all your life? Your father. So please, listen to me now. Don't marry that man. You could stand here for a year and a day, and I still wouldn't give you my blessings.

"I love you. I do. But believe me when I say that there are better things out there for you. I didn't send you to school in England so you could learn all that Greek, Latin and French and then throw it all away by marrying him."

Evelyn, cheeks moistened with tears, pulled away from her father's grasp with a shrug of her shoulder. "You don't understand, Dad. You never did. What does my education have anything to do with it? Charles is educated. He's nobility. He's everything that a proud father could want for her daughter. But you refuse to see that and now here you are, raging for all the world's worth, and unable to see how happy he makes me and how much I love him."

"He's Catholic, Evelyn. Jesus, a Catholic. Do you know what the people would say? Do you? Do you have any idea?" Byrd walked over to his bar and from a crystal decanter poured out a glass of whiskey. He sipped the deep

Westover Plantation in Richmond, Virginia

brown liquid, felt its warmth in the pit of his belly. "You've already seen how they've abandoned you. How all your friends shun you now, avoiding you as if you were a leper."

He sighed. "Why do you want to make things difficult for yourself? I've spent my life trying to give you all the conveniences and advantages that you could possibly want and now, with a will that could only have come from your mother, you want to throw that all away.

"Your mother and I have made every effort to be patient, yet still you persist. Haven't we introduced you to countless other eligible suitors who would meet with our approval? Men from good families, good Protestant families. Men who share our values and yours. Yet you turned each and every one of them away. You spurned them all and continue to soil the good name I've given you."

"Father, how many times must I tell you this?" Evelyn asked, exasperated. It was a conversation she'd had too many times before. "I don't love them. I love one man and one man alone. And I will always love him. Don't you see? I don't care if my friends have abandoned me. If they're willing to do so because of Charles, then I don't want them for friends. Besides, Anne has always stayed true. What more could I possibly need or want?"

Byrd snorted, drank some more from his snifter. "Yes, Anne. The Carter-Harrisons have done a magnificent job raising that one. Has she nothing better to do than meet you in that grove by Westover day in and day out?"

Evelyn resisted the urge to challenge her father. It had already been too long a day. The sun was beginning to sink beneath the horizon, and she could feel the chill of evening creeping its way across the land. The wind rustled in the leaves, and as the sun's light grew ever fainter and the darkness and warmth of the library ever more claustrophobic, she hung her head. She knew then, as she must have known all along, that her father would never yield. He would never relent. Her love for Charles Morduant had been doomed from the start, yet somewhere along the way, as she entered the summer of her life with Charles in her arm, she let herself believe that perhaps she had underestimated her father. It pained her now to know that she estimated her father perfectly.

She sighed and ran her hand through her hair. Her father stood by his desk, shuffling uncomfortably from one foot to the other. How he hated the silence, Evelyn thought to herself. But she didn't want to speak. If she did, the talk would be over and so too would her relationship. So she stood there, looking out the window to the James River. She thought of Charles in London. What would he be doing now? Most likely he would be asleep, his face that of an angel's.

The silence was almost overpowering. All that broke it was the ticking of the grandfather clock in the hallway, the time between each tick and tock seeming to get longer and longer. Occasionally, the floorboards creaked and Evelyn knew that her father had shifted his stance again. Finally, she spoke.

"All right, Father. I can do no more. I feel as if I've talked myself blue in the face. Charles and I will not see each other again."

Byrd put down his glass and walked over to his daughter. He opened his arms, ready to embrace her.

"You've made me a happy father," he said. "You have, Evelyn."

She pushed him away and her eyes flashed with an intensity and a rage that Byrd had never seen before. "Don't touch me, Father. You might be happy, but what about me? I don't want a thing from you."

She stormed out of the room and it was at that moment that people say that Evelyn was changed forever. No one ever saw her again in the city of Richmond, Virginia. Denied love by a cruel and unforgiving society, Evelyn decided that she would deny them all that she had

Evelyn Byrd shut herself inside Westover after her love affair with Charles Morduant ended.

left: herself. She shut herself up in the family mansion at Westover Plantation, and only a few ever caught a glimpse of the heartbroken girl as she walked across the front lawn, passing in and out of the shadows of the 150-year-old tulip poplars, like a wraith on her way to the James River to meet with Anne.

These daily meetings with her dearest, closest friend were all that Evelyn had to anticipate. Her father was at a loss to reach her, yet still he would not offer the one thing he knew would bring the life back to his daughter's step. His pride would not allow it. He convinced himself that Evelyn would get better, that she would begin to venture off Westover Plantation and begin to live her life again. But it was not to be; Charles had left her life, and darkness stepped into the void. Evelyn remained distant, and no amount of coaxing or baiting by her mother or father could reach her. She emerged only to talk to Anne, the one person who had never turned her back on her.

Even after November 1737, Anne still went down to the grove by the James River, a dedication all the more impressive when it's revealed that Evelyn died in that month and that year.

Doctors never found a cause for Evelyn's death, and her passing remained a mystery. But those who knew her best—Anne and her parents—knew deep inside that Anne had died from a broken heart. Anne cursed the parents under her breath, condemning them for their clouded judgments that blinded them to the needs of their daughter. Anne wept for her friend, remembering the last words her dearest had uttered to her.

"I'm dying, Anne," Evelyn had said as they watched the sun set along the banks of the James.

Anne just laughed, but she couldn't help noticing how sickly her friend looked, how wan and pale her complexion was. "Don't be silly, Ev. You'll be with us for a long while yet."

Evelyn ignored her. The tone in Anne's voice betrayed her; Anne knew that Evelyn spoke the truth. "Promise me one thing, dear Anne."

"Anything."

"Meet me here every day. Even after my death. I shall come to meet you as always."

Anne pledged her word, and days later, received news that at the age of 29, Evelyn had died.

Anne continued to wait by the grove for her dead friend. Nothing, it seemed, not even death, could keep these close companions apart. Anne could only watch, mouth agape, as a figure dressed in brilliant white stepped lightly across the grass to the grove. The deep brown of the girl's hair and the blue eyes left no doubt in Anne's mind that her friend had managed to keep a promise.

Those concerned that Evelyn wouldn't have company in the afterlife needn't have worried. Evelyn's was not the only life to have been cut tragically short at Westover.

Her brother and his wife both suffered early deaths and have accompanied their relative into the ghostly afterlife. But while Evelyn's spirit swore in life that she would return in a form that all would find pleasing, her relatives made no such claims.

Many people have been fooled by Evelyn's appearance. She is still stunning and has been seen, dressed in her shimmering white dress, throughout the years, combing her hair in a mirror, hovering over slumbering children and walking the steps leading from the kitchen to the pantry. And of course, out on the lawn on moonlit nights when she appears like a light in the darkness.

Whenever she is seen, she appears as a three-dimensional figure, and most people who see her aren't even aware that she's a ghost until she vanishes from sight, evaporating like a breath on a windowpane.

It is the other spirits who have terrified the staff and residents of Westover Plantation. Elizabeth Hill Carter Byrd was Evelyn's sister-in-law and she entered a marriage that her mother-in-law never approved of. Just as they had been relentless in ending Evelyn's relationship with Charles, so too did the Byrds attempt to make their son's marriage as difficult as possible for their daughter-in-law. It seems that some lessons are never learned.

Moriah Byrd could be cruel and vindictive if one happened to fall out of her favor. Elizabeth was one such unfortunate soul. Moriah constantly assaulted Elizabeth's fragile constitution, playing upon the younger girl's fears and concerns about her husband. After all, it was rumored that William Byrd III was far from loyal with his affections for his wife, and while Elizabeth was usually able to put these nagging doubts about her husband's fidelity out of her mind, Moriah's constant claims that her son never loved Elizabeth wore on her like water washing over rock. Moriah was determined to drive Elizabeth away and she hit upon a scheme.

William kept a chest, high above on another chest. It was always locked, and its contents remained a secret to Elizabeth. She'd always wondered what lay inside, and Moriah told her one sad day that it held the love letters of all her husband's mistresses. Elizabeth couldn't resist the temptation to learn the truth about her husband. And if Moriah was wrong, then perhaps she would desist and give her a moment's peace. If she was right, then at least she could begin to deal with the truth.

To get to the chest, Elizabeth had to climb the large piece of furniture. She did, but as she clambered up the

Evelyn's melancholy ghost, one of several spirits in the historic home, appears in various rooms.

structure, it began to rock and then sway. Then it crashed upon her helpless body. She died instantly, but her screams still echoed in and around the room. Moriah was devastated when she discovered what had happened, or at the very least, appeared to be, for no one will ever know if Moriah intended for the "accident" to happen. One assumes that she didn't, for she is reported to have spent her last years lamenting and regretting her machinations.

Elizabeth died, but something of her spirit remains at Westover. She doesn't appear to people, but few can miss her screams as they continue to issue forth from the room in which she was crushed.

As for her husband, it seems as if the rumors about his philandering might have been true. Despite losing his wife and the mother of his five children, William Byrd III married again just six months after Elizabeth's death. And even though the second marriage was, by all accounts, a happy one, he could not keep his other demons at bay. His love of gambling led him to lose his entire fortune, and having lost the family plantation, William took his own life with poison. His body was found slumped against an armchair in his bedroom.

People who slept in that room found sleep elusive. Their attempts at slumber were haunted at all hours by a chilling presence that filled the entire room. Those who descended from the room the next morning, exhausted and sick with fear, swore that they had felt the icy grip of death itself.

But for 300 years, the woman who had lived a life in complete denial of what she wanted and in complete servitude to her parents has haunted the mansion in which she spent so many of her tortured years, with no one for company but her best friend, Anne. It's a mystery why Evelyn Byrd continues to live in the mansion that must have been the scene of so much distress, but questions aside, Evelyn seems at long last to be happy. Whenever her spirit is seen, it is with a smile on her face.

Miss Elizabeth
TEMPLE HEIGHTS, MISSISSIPPI

The boy was new to Columbus, Mississippi. He'd just moved to the city and had spent his first few days exploring its avenues and alleys. Summer was dwindling, and he was determined to experience all of Columbus' mysteries and secrets before the long, sun-drenched days came to an end.

This day, he'd gotten out of bed determined to make it to Temple Heights. He hadn't made too many friends yet, but every kid he'd talked to always made some crack about the crazy lady who lived in Temple Heights. They'd laugh boldly when they talked about how she was so crazy that no one wanted to marry her, that she hated all men and tormented little boys with her cackle if they even approached the house.

Sure, he'd known kooks and eccentrics where he'd grown up, but he'd never heard of a woman who used chalk dust to render her face an alarming shade of pale and then contrasted its blinding white with the brilliant orange of Mercurochrome that she used as lipstick and rouge. Her hair, he heard, had been dyed as red as the fires of hell. From a distance, kids had told him, she looked like a flaming matchstick. Up close, she was like some sort of demented clown.

"I don't know. Maybe she escaped from the circus," the kids had said and then, pausing as their faces contorted themselves into cruel grins, they continued, "or was set loose."

The day was warm and humid, and as he walked to the house, the boy was surprised to realize how quickly his heart was beating and how clammy his hands had gotten despite the heat. He told himself to calm down, to remember that those kids with their stories might know some things and what they didn't know they'd make up. He turned a corner and there it was—Temple Heights. It was a beautiful mansion, he thought. Gleaming white with 3 porches (he counted), 14 columns and 4 floors. He marveled at its magnificence and thought that surely everything he'd heard was nothing but lies. Crazy people didn't live in houses like this, did they? They lived under bridges and in lean-tos, just like the trolls he'd read about in fairy tales.

He laughed, wondering why he'd been so scared. He strolled by the house once and then again, his head bobbing up and down as he tried to catch a glimpse of what lay behind the mansion's pristine windows. He saw nothing as the sun was bright and the windows may as well have been mirrors. He could only see his head bobbing up and down like an apple in a tub. Squinting into the sun, he decided to wait.

He wasn't there long when he heard the creak of the front door. First he saw the shoe, and then the long hoop skirt, neither of which was unusual. And then he saw what had frightened so many of the children around the neighborhood. She was exactly as they described. His breath froze in his throat and his heart raced. Run away, he commanded his legs, but they seemed to be rooted to the walk. He was staring, and he knew it, yet he couldn't turn away. Everything he had heard was true. It wasn't until the woman turned to him and raised her hand by way of greeting that he regained muscle control. The boy let out a little yelp and then ran, fleeing down the street as fast as his young legs could carry him.

When he'd run three or four blocks, he stopped on shaky legs, gasping for air. He couldn't believe it. He'd actually seen the ghost of Temple Heights. How cool was that, he asked himself. As he walked the rest of the way home, forgetting his fear with each step, he knew that he would never forget what he had seen and couldn't wait to tell his brothers all about it.

His curiosity led him to seek out the identity of the apparition; it was a painstaking process, but he finally uncovered for himself what he thought might be the story behind the ghost at Temple Heights. It turned out that the woman's name was Miss Elizabeth Kennebrew, and she had lived in the house in the late 1880s. She came to the house with her Methodist minister father, J. H. Kennebrew, who had bought the house in 1887. The original owners were the Brownriggs of North Carolina, and Temple Heights had been built as an exact replica of Mrs. Brownrigg's previous home.

The Kennebrews had five daughters: Daisy, Laura, Jessie, Ruth and Elizabeth. Those were pretty names, the boy thought. He wondered if they had been pretty in life; after all, he found it strange that when their father died, he left a will that said the house could not be sold until all five girls were married. Was he intent on keeping the house and knew that there was no way that all five of his daughters would ever marry? Or did he think that the condition would inspire his girls to go out and seek the company of others?

In the end, only two of the sisters found husbands. The other three lived out their lives in Temple Heights, and as the years passed, Elizabeth acquired a reputation as the strangest of them all. The boy smiled. No doubt it had something to do with her choice of makeup. He didn't know what Mercurochrome was, so he had to ask his parents. When they told him it was something like iodine, he winced.

Miss Elizabeth died in 1965, but she didn't go far. Carl and Dixie Butler, dedicated historical conservationists, bought the home to preserve and restore its legacy. Through their work, Temple Heights was designated a Mississippi Landmark, placed on the National Register and decorated with museum-quality objects that suggest that the 19th century is alive and well in the mansion. When the Butlers first moved into the house, they were the audience for a symphony of sounds whose conductor remained safely anonymous. The sounds they heard were the tinkles and crashes normally associated with breaking glass and slamming windows, but the Butlers never found any shards of glass, and their windows were always open.

Noise wasn't the only sign of an otherworldly presence in the house. The Butlers were mystified when they walked up the stairs and found the old rocking chair rocking as if there were someone sitting in it. When Mr. Butler was cleaning one of the bedroom doors, he frowned and became puzzled. Didn't the door have the name Laura carved into it? He was sure it did and now the grain was smooth and polished, untouched. The name had disappeared.

Sometimes the Butlers heard their names whispered when the house was empty. And the chair still rocked. The glasses cracked. The windows slammed. All without any spirit ever announcing his or her presence—until the day a guest staying in the house saw something pass her on the stairs. When it did, she felt very cold and shivered. She looked at the figure and saw her face. She gasped and went down to tell the Butlers about the apparition she'd seen vanish on the top floor. The face could be none other than that of Miss Elizabeth Kennebrew.

The boy, though frightened when he first saw the apparition, returned eagerly to Temple Heights when he learned that it would be open for spring and summer tours. He could learn all about the house from its guides and maybe, if he was lucky enough, he would catch a glimpse of Miss Elizabeth and he could apologize for running off when they'd first met. After all, the Butlers have had nothing but good things to say about the spirit with whom they continue to share their mansion. The boy looked forward to returning.

Who Do Voodoo?
NEW ORLEANS, LOUISIANA

"She's the devil, she is."

"A pagan destined for eternal damnation. She'll be going straight to hell."

"You'll stay away from her if you know what's good for you."

Marie Laveau had heard it all throughout her life. But suspicion and derision were to be expected of people whose understanding of her culture, her beliefs and her religion was scattered at best. There were those in New Orleans, however, who looked to Laveau for guidance and direction and who believed in her powers of voodoo. Indeed, there are those today in New Orleans who still do. They believe the myths and legends that surrounded her existence, and that she died looking much as she had in her 20s. Even her death in 1881 has not kept Marie Laveau from leaving her tomb to lead those to the bayou on St. John's Eve.

Marie Laveau drew sidelong glances and whispers because she was a powerful woman, who, unlike the slaves who worked the plantations, could not be controlled or dictated to. The daughter of a white man and a black slave, Laveau was born in 1794, free from the shackles of slavery. She had been born in what is now Haiti and it was there where she was first initiated into the rites and rituals of voodoo.

Voodoo originated in Haiti, a result of European attempts to keep slaves segregated. Slaves from different

Two Marie Laveaus are buried but by no means confined in St. Louis Cemetery No.1 in New Orleans.

ethnic backgrounds were put together, the idea being that having been deprived of their freedom and culture, they would now be deprived further of their community, language and identity. But their Europeans masters failed; the slaves had their shackles in common. They shared their disdain for their white masters. Theirs was a language made familiar through misery and oppression.

Though they had been baptized as Roman Catholics upon their arrival in Haiti and other West Indian islands, the slaves were able to practice their old religions. Slaves from groups such as the Fon, the Nago, Congos, Senegalese, Libyans, Ethiopians, Caplaous and Hassaurs continued to practice their different faiths within their multi-ethnic communities. Rituals became mingled and were modified until the religion recognized today as voodoo was born, its name derived from a West African word for spirit.

The religion, needless to say, frightened and confused the Protestant and Roman Catholic slaveholders. Its rituals and rites were strange and unusual, and, fearful that their own might be misled into joining what they could only call a cult, they began to spread rumors and speculation that fueled many of the misconceptions regarding voodoo today.

"It's barbaric," they said. "A primitive belief based on nothing but sex, superstition and spectacle." A number of their houngans and mambos, priests of the order, were arrested and hanged, driving the religion further underground, where it was forced to adopt elements of Christianity.

Into this era of intolerance and oppression walked Marie Laveau. She had arrived in New Orleans in 1819, where she married Jacques Paris. He died only seven years later, and shortly after she married Christophe Glapion. The first of 15 children was born and Marie gave the child her own name.

Marie's reputation grew quickly, and she became a leading figure for the oppressed. She took an active interest in slaves sentenced to death by hanging for a variety of crimes. Her power was such that judges and policemen fell under her spell, releasing slaves upon her command. People were mystified at her abilities and whispered that she must have charmed the authorities. Most failed to put the pieces of the puzzle together. Marie was a powerful mambo with a charisma and beauty few could resist. But to support herself, Marie and her daughter Marie became hairdressers, catering to the wealthy and the social elite, dressed in garb far different than what she wore down in the bayou.

No one noticed her as she cut and styled hair. Her clients gossiped freely about whatever scandals were percolating through the social strata that week. Marie listened the entire time, and considering that men are slaves to their vices, she was able to glean enough information to buy the freedom of those who weren't given a chance to speak for themselves.

Marie also gathered people on the banks of Lake Ponchartrain at St. John's Bayou for bonfire rituals. The rites, which went well into the evening, kept a nervous city awake as they watched the shadows dance in the firelight, smoke rising high in the air. No one knows exactly what took place at Laveau's gatherings, but people were certain that it involved dancing nude, orgies and animal sacrifices. Of course, their suspicions might not have been very far from the truth, but while they believed that the slaves and their Voodoo Queen were practicing dark magic and evil sorcery, Marie was only leading them in

The ghosts of Marie and her daughter are known to lead a group of ghosts to St. John's Bayou, where they practice voodoo.

the rituals that were meant to help its followers acquire more food, a better living and improved health. To be sure, there were those who practiced the dark arts, but Marie Laveau was not one of them.

Suspicion only heightened when people began to realize that Marie seemed blessed with perpetual youth.

Those who remembered her arriving in New Orleans in the late 18th century marveled that even decades later, she still looked as youthful as ever. The years had been impossibly kind to her exquisite features. It wasn't until she died that people realized it hadn't been Marie Laveau. It was her daughter who had assumed her mother's role when the latter died in 1881. So alike were the two that few noticed any difference between them. The truth of the matter is affirmed by the existence of two tombs in New Orleans' St. Louis Cemetery No. 1 bearing the name Marie Laveau. As ghosts, the two are distinguished by the elder Marie's tignon, a seven-knotted handkerchief which she never took off.

Both of them have been seen walking from their tombs to lead a horde of ghosts to St. John's Bayou, where they continue to engage in voodoo practices. If the walk is too much or the weather is inclement, the spirits return to her house on St. Ann Street, where Marie's spirit, clad in her tignon and a long white dress, leads her followers in voodoo ceremonies. On days when she needs her rest, she walks the streets alone, observing everything around her. She walks to the St. John's Bayou where her voice can be heard, singing songs of freedom and hope.

6
Jails and Forts

Sturdivant Hall
SELMA, ALABAMA

When Mr. and Mrs. Robert Sturdivant donated $50,000 to the community of Selma, they wanted their money to help develop a showcase for their collection of antiques. Today Sturdivant Hall bears their name because of their generosity. But there's more on display in the house than the Sturdivants' stellar collection. The house is known as much for the continued presence of a man who died in 1867 as for its unique Southern furniture. John McGee Parkman may have lived in the house for only two years, but if anyone were to still call Sturvidant home, it would be Parkman.

Sturdivant Hall was built on a lot that Edward T. Watts had bought for $1830 at a public sale. He hired Thomas Helm Lee, a cousin of Confederate general Robert E. Lee, to design and construct the neoclassical mansion. After a year, Watts had his home, erected at a cost of $69,000. Watts lived there with his wife, Louisa, for 12 years before he decided to sell the property.

Elias Parkman arrived in Selma in 1817. His son John was born in 1838. John turned out to be a prodigy of sorts, a hard-working and dedicated industrialist who started out selling dry goods and then progressed from clerk to bookkeeper to bank teller to cashier. In 1866, he was named president of the First National Bank of Selma and entrusted with capital totaling over $100,000. Two years earlier, he had bought the Watts property for $65,000. Just 28 years old, John seemed as close to happiness as one

Sturdivant Hall in Selma, Alabama

could get. How could he have known that within a year he would lose everything he had spent his life working for?

Shortly after he was named bank president, a man came to meet John at his office. The man presented himself as General Wager Swayne, commander of the federal troops stationed in Selma. He announced that John was being placed under arrest, and that the bank and its assets were now under his control. John could only stare incredulously at the general. He believed that he had always acted with integrity and honesty as did the people who knew him.

General Swayne was dismayed to learn that John, like so many others at commercial houses, had used bank capital to speculate on cotton. The investment proved unwise. While many others who had been guilty of the same act did not go to jail, the glaring difference in John's case was that the United States government had large deposits of money in the bank. John had lost these, making his arrest a necessity. Protest as they might, John's family could not convince Swayne of John's innocence. He was arrested, convicted and thrown into a Confederate prison at Cahaba.

But John wasn't without his allies. Family members and friends conspired to free him and, on the appointed night, arrived at Cahaba. A guard was bribed to leave John's cell door open. He slipped out under the cover of darkness, made his way past the prison walls and was almost at the river when a guard in a watchtower spotted the fleeing prisoner. He gave John a warning, but it went unheeded. Parkman was so close to the riverboat destined for Selma that he refused to surrender. Freedom, he felt, was within his grasp.

The guard fired once, twice. John fell into the river, dead. His wife, with no income, was forced to sell the home, at a loss, for $12,000. John Parkman was buried in Live Oak Cemetery—or at least his body was. The same can't be said of his spirit. His family might have moved on, but John wasn't quite ready to abandon his Selma house.

The Gillmans bought the home and it remained in their family until 1957, when the city of Selma bought the home for $75,000. To purchase the house, the city used $50,000 from the estate of the late Robert Sturdivant, whose will had provided for the creation of a museum in Selma. One wonders now if Sturdivant had meant a living museum.

John returned to what is now Sturdivant Hall and has haunted the building for years. His apparition has been seen looking out from the cupola at the top of the house. Visitors and volunteers at the museum report that his presence can be felt in an upstairs bedroom as well as the downstairs parlor.

One time, concerned neighbors summoned the police to the property when they saw windows and doors opening and closing on their own. Officers forced their way into the building only to discover that nothing was amiss. All the doors and windows were securely fastened and, most curious of all, the building was empty. Firefighters were just as puzzled when they were called out to Sturdivant Hall because concerned citizens had seen smoke billowing out from the upstairs windows. There might have been smoke, but there was definitely no fire, leaving a squad of confused firefighters.

Pat Tate has written about her experiences in Sturdivant Hall. She has heard on numerous occasions phantom footsteps moving across the second floor of the house. She has seen doors open and close on their own and has found beds in disarray when, just moments earlier, they were neatly made. Whenever the doors open, Tate greets Parkman, saying "Good evening."

The mansion was the venue for a ball that followed a reenactment of the Battle of Selma. People were stationed at the staircases to make sure that no one mistakenly wandered upstairs, an area restricted to museum staff. Tate

The downstairs parlor is one of several areas where museum volunteers have seen the apparition of John Parkman.

noticed that one of the people had abandoned his post. When he returned, Tate questioned him as to where he had gone. The guard claimed that he had gone upstairs to investigate three reports of children looking out the window. He found nothing except empty rooms.

Once, an exterminator had been spraying the rooms upstairs when he felt a strange sensation, a feeling that someone was pushing him from behind. He raced down the stairs and out of the house, pledging never to return again. In other corners of the house, witnesses have seen rocking chairs rock on their own, while a group of children were startled when a painting set on an easel appeared to leap off and shatter into a hundred pieces. The children were not nearly as rattled as one might have thought; after all, they knew that it was just John Parkman making his presence felt.

Sturdivant Hall is listed on the National Register of Historic Places. Its collection of period furniture, portraits, silver, dolls and toys recreate the antebellum South, allowing visitors to step back in time. The home is still regarded as one of the most beautiful homes in the Southeast. John McGee Parkman surely must agree.

Castillo de San Marcos
ST. AUGUSTINE, FLORIDA

"Isn't it beautiful, Delores? Castillo de San Marcos. Magnificent. Why, do you know that it has never been taken by any army? Its walls have withstood countless blasts of cannon and, look, still they stand." Colonel Garcia Marti was itching to get off the galleon. He'd seen the fort gleaming on the coast for over a day now. As the galleon had approached the Florida coast, he had pulled out his telescope to catch a glimpse of the fort. He was close enough now that all he had to do was squint and put away the telescope. He drank the air down, savoring its aromas and tastes. "We are almost home, Delores." If Colonel Garcia Marti had known what would happen just

Castillo de San Marcos in Florida was the first permanent European settlement in the United States.

months after his arrival, he probably would have ordered the ship to return to Spain. In a short while, he would be stripped of his rank, be an embarrassment to the army and be a murderer of not just one, but two people. The echoes of his crime are still heard today in the Castillo de San Marcos.

Delores squinted and shielded her eyes from the sun with her hand. She was proud of her husband, but moving to St. Augustine did not appeal to her. Everything that she had known and loved had been left behind in Spain and now, on the cusp of a grand adventure, all she wanted was to turn the ship around and head back to Spain. Marti's appointment had come after years of dedicated service and who was she to question his acceptance of the commission now? She loved her husband, but she had grown anxious when he warned her that his new posting meant that he would be busy, keeping long and late hours that would keep the two of them apart. The two settled into life at the fort, but Delores still found the adjustment difficult. Duties were constantly taking Marti away from her, and when they did have a free moment, he was too exhausted and weary for even light conversation. Delores was lonely.

When she had first arrived at the fort, Delores was introduced to Captain Manuel Abela, her husband's chief officer. As the chief officer, he attended to Marti's needs and, by extension, Delores' needs too. When she had taken his hand in greeting, she hadn't failed to notice how charming and handsome Abela was. Charged with her care while Marti was at work, Abela began spending many hours with the colonel's wife.

For Delores, what had initially started as a respectful friendship with her husband's chief officer had blossomed into something more, something with the potential to destroy everything that existed between her and her husband. But the affair flourished, sheltered as they were by Marti's dedication to work. Yet, every night as

Delores lay in bed next to her husband, she wept with shame, almost disbelieving what she had done. She told herself that she would end it soon, that nothing good could possibly come out of her infidelity, but as the sun rose and the light of day met her eyes, everything became clouded again. Reason told her what she needed to do, but her heart refused to yield, despite her best attempts to end the relationship.

Marti was oblivious to everything for a while; he might have noticed that Delores had been behaving differently if only he could spare some of his attention for his wife. Eventually he realized something was amiss. It was a small thing, which was probably why Abela had neglected to notice. Inured now by routine and complacency, Abela was no longer as vigilant about his appearance or clothing and neglected to change his shirt after an afternoon with Delores.

As the two men stood in Marti's office, looking over maps, Abela pointed out a position but Marti, in the dim light, had to lean in to make out the coordinates. He pressed close against Abela as he tried to get a better look and it was then that he caught the unmistakable scent of his wife. He wondered if she had walked into his office. He sniffed again, and realized that the smell was on his first officer.

Marti's heart trembled and something inside that mind snapped. How could he have been so blind? How could he have been so ignorant? Everything was so obvious and clear now. Marti's mind was fixed now on one single purpose: revenge. While he said nothing to Abela, he had already decided that he would catch the two of

Today, the spirits of Delores and Manuel, two adulterous lovers slain by Delores' jealous husband, linger in the gloomy dungeon.

them together and then watch as they tried to explain themselves before he brought their deaths down upon them.

No one ever questioned the colonel's reasons for Abela's and Maria's subsequent disappearances. Abela, he had said, had been called back suddenly to Spain to serve there. Delores, he had said, was ill, and had gone to

Mexico to recover under the watchful eyes of her relatives. Why was there any reason to doubt the colonel?

Fifty years later, in 1834, the fort had passed into American hands after the United States had purchased Florida from the Spanish in 1821. It was then that the true extent of Colonel Garcia Marti's crimes came to light. An excavation of the dungeons revealed a room long forgotten. When its sealed door was pried open by American soldiers, they found ash and skeletal remains within. Were these the bodies of Delores and Abela?

A national monument now, Castillo de San Marcos holds fast as the first permanent European settlement in the United States. Tourists walk its halls, and when they pass through the dungeon, they quickly leave, convinced that something of the two lovers' spirits still linger in the gloom. The scent of perfume fills the room, accompanied by a faint glow, and Castillo de San Marcos comes to life once more with the presence of two murdered souls.

Fort St. Simons
ST. SIMONS ISLAND, GEORGIA

The transformation of America began with the arrival of the first Europeans. Greed for the wealth that lay in pelts, crops and minerals led to the establishment of a number of colonies, which had little regard for the indigenous peoples who already lived on the earth and who had established communion with the lands they inhabited. Diseases such as tuberculosis began to kill off the aboriginals, who had neither the knowledge nor immunity to fight illnesses that had never been seen on their shores. And what illness did not do was accomplished through warfare and treaties whose terms were never meant to be fulfilled. Few settlers cared about the systematic genocide of tribes such as the Cherokee, the Sioux, the Iroquois, the Huron and the Seminole as long as they were able to take their land and earn a living.

Dissension, however, arose in some new arrivals, men who believed that colonization was an affront to the aboriginals and who believed that they should return to Europe. One in particular continues to speak for the oppressed, and while the world of the native Americans receded long ago into folklore, myth and legend, Dr. Christian Priber continues to speak out against the European presence on Georgia's St. Simons Island. The remarkable part of it all, of course, is that Dr. Priber has been dead since at least the late 18th century. But still, late at night, Dr. Priber can be heard speaking. He was multilingual, but the voices heard are in languages other than English.

Christian Priber, an idiosyncratic 18th-century doctor, created a utopian community in the Smoky Mountains.

Dr. Christian Priber came from Germany to Charleston, South Carolina, in 1736. His position granted him easy access to the most vaunted social circles and he was able to remain there through his charm, grace and intelligence. Few who met him could resist the good doctor.

There is little evidence to explain how Dr. Priber disappeared one day, taking with him nothing but the leather-bound chest in which he kept the writings that he had hoped to one day turn into a book. For months, people wondered what had happened to Dr. Priber. His vanishing act captured the city's attention, and rumors about the disappearance swirled as thick and heavy as the mists that rolled in off the South Carolina coast. Had the savages who roamed the wilderness captured him? Had he been killed? Had he fled to Europe? What would cause a man to abandon his life? An examination of his house revealed little, adding only more to the mystery of his disappearance. Everything was in order, suggesting there was no struggle, that he'd disappeared of his own volition.

People despaired of ever learning the truth, and the mystery faded from conversation as Charleston settled back into routine. Priber's disappearance would simply remain one of those unexplained twists of fate. Soon, though, the state of South Carolina was filled with whispers of a strange man who had appeared in the Smoky Mountains accompanied by Cherokee. He was deemed strange because he was obviously European and was apparently determined to establish a government of his own in which the European settlers would be expelled from their lands. The strange man seemed highly educated in both literature and science and he spoke many languages. Those who heard the stories in Charleston couldn't help thinking that the descriptions matched very closely with those of Dr. Priber, but they had trouble believing the good doctor would behave so oddly. As it turned out, Charleston knew little about Dr. Priber.

Shortly thereafter, a letter was delivered via Indian courier to the mansion of Governor William Bull from what apparently was a newly created country: the Republic of Paradise. A new government had been formed and it demanded that anyone not willing to swear its loyalty to the regime leave the country at once. Bull shook his head, wondering what sort of foolishness had come over the Cherokee this time. He was ready to toss the letter into the garbage when he noticed the named signed at the bottom was none other than that of Christian Priber, Prime Minister.

Governor Bull sent the letter to the governor of Georgia and the two decided that something had to be done, that Priber seemed bent on leading an Indian insurrection. The relative security and peace of the colonies were under threat. Troops were ordered to scour the Smoky Mountains and place Priber under arrest for treason. The directive was simple, but carrying it out proved far more difficult than they expected.

Before the troops could even reach the Smoky Mountains, Cherokee scouts intercepted them and brought them before Priber. While the scouts were in favor of killing the invaders, Priber knew that to do so would be to invite many more. He stayed their hands and sent the men back to their governors where the red-faced troops described how it was indeed Priber who was presiding over the Republic of Paradise. He had married a Cherokee woman, spoke the language ably and had even written a dictionary of the language. The men described how Priber had tried to persuade them to join his country, claiming that it was to be a utopia on earth.

Unlike the colonies, everything would be communal. Wealth and poverty would both be eliminated, as all property would be distributed equally. Women would not be looked down upon as inferior and would be allowed to own property and to vote. No one would want for anything in the republic. It was a far cry from the industrialized world of the Europeans and its stratified social classes.

Still, Governor Bull shook his head. Priber was a fugitive who would be brought to justice. But Priber remained elusive, avoiding the men charged with bringing him in. For five years he lived in his republic, until the day he decided that he would offer peace to the Creek Indians. With an escort of Cherokee braves, he made his way to Creek Indian lands with his leather-bound chest in tow. It was his last trip. The colonials had learned about the trip and planned an ambush. Priber was captured after a brief skirmish and taken to the prison barracks at Fort St. Simons on St. Simons Island.

No one knows how long Priber remained in the prison barracks. He died in custody and the Republic of Paradise died with him. The dream, though, lives on. During his time in prison, Priber spoke to anyone who would listen—and there were many—about the republic. He continued to write, filling up the leather-bound chest with his manuscript. It's not known exactly what Priber was writing, but those who saw pages of it were certain it had to do with the republic.

Even now, in the shadow of night in the prison barracks, Priber still speaks to anyone who would listen. His is a dream that gains greater currency in a world where the rich get richer and the poor get poorer.

7
Supernatural Nature

Okefenokee Swamp
GEORGIA

It is a tale older than history, told many times before European explorers ever set foot upon the North American continent. It is a piece of Indian folklore, a story existing between myth and legend. It is a land of magic, riddled with swamps, bogs and mystery. It is known as the largest swamp in North America, but the Indians who crossed the waters of the Okefenokee Swamp cared not for its magnitude or size. They came to it because it haunted their dreams. They came to it because it called to them with the voices of the ethereal, with the promise of the tantalizing unknown and with the possibility for a realm beyond any sort of imagining. For deep within the murk and mist of the swamp lay an island paradise, home to a race of women whose grace and beauty were legendary.

In 2500 BC, aboriginals inhabited the Okefenokee Swamp. The names of these peoples were the Deptfords, the Swift Creek and the Weeden Island. Even then, the bogs were a mysterious place, a land that existed somewhere between earth and water. Death was not uncommon here, as the bog was known to swallow people whole if they were not careful to watch where they trod. It must have mystified the people when they realized that bodies trapped in the bog did not rot and decay as they might have somewhere else. They could not explain it; they only knew that the tea-colored waters of the Okefenokee Swamp were magical.

The Okefenokee Swamp in southeastern Georgia has fascinated people for hundreds of years.

The floor of the swamp was covered in an earth that could be cut and dried to use in fires. As the rich earth was slow burning, it could be buried one night and used to ignite another fire the following day. The land was sacred, blessed by some great spirit. It had to be. The tribes marveled at how the land shook and trembled when they stomped on the ground, causing trees and bushes to sway. Surely, here was evidence of some great power.

It's not known exactly when the stories started, but as the swamp was explored, groups came back with accounts of strange women inhabiting an island paradise deep in the heart of the swamp. As the sun lay low upon the horizon, shrouding the land in mist, Native Indians watched with awe as figures crossed the bog, gliding across the treacherous lands with ease. Their voices were instruments whose music, sound and melodies had never been heard before. They spoke not in words but in lyrics. Some were moved to tears as they felt their hearts touched in ways they never knew possible. Others closed their eyes, trembling as the sensations of everything that is pure and noble rippled through their bodies. Yet no matter how long people searched the swamp that covered 400,000 acres, they never found the elusive paradise. They often returned with their numbers reduced, but always with renewed hope as they regaled the others with fresh accounts of what they had seen.

And so the legend grew. Older generations passed the stories on to the youth, who set off again into the peat to succeed where their ancestors had failed. As the years passed, the legend only grew in size. But the island remained only a destination of the imagination. The young fantasized about the island's beauty, speaking with wide-eyed optimism about a land free of death, suffering and any hardship. No wonder, then, that when the Europeans arrived in the 16th century, they too began seeking the island utopia.

"It's in the Okefenokee," the Spanish said. "It's there in the land of the trembling earth."

Success lay beyond their grasp, but the less successful they were, the more persistent they became. The settlers continued to enter the swamp, sometimes harried by Seminole Indians who saw their invasion as a threat to the security of their homes. Death found the settlers often, yet still they came in even greater numbers, until finally the Seminole Indians were driven out during the Second Seminole War by General Charles R. Floyd.

The swamp was now the Europeans' to explore for the presence of the Fatchaksia, the name the women had been given in the lands now called the Okefenokee National Wildlife Refuge. Its mysteries have long been solved. The way it preserved bodies? Tannic acids in the water from decaying vegetation choked out the oxygen in the slow-moving water, preventing the bodies from rotting while they tanned the skin black. The rich soil that burned for so long was peat, which lay 15 feet thick in some parts of the swamp.

The swamp had once been part of the ocean floor and emptied itself into the Gulf of Mexico and the Atlantic Ocean. As American settlements of the lands increased, much of the swamp was drained to fuel the Southern economies of Georgia and used to plant rice, sugar cane and cotton. When these ventures failed, the lands were cleared of timber for logging. It was only in 1937 that the American government stepped in to preserve the lands that had sustained Indian cultures for millenia and that the Americans were threatening to destroy in less than a century. The lands were precious not only as a place of folklore but also as a valuable ecosystem that was home to such birds as loons, egrets, ibises and cranes. But is it still home to the Fatchaksia? Hunters and fishermen, trolling the waters of Okefenokee, have seen what thousands of others had seen before them. They see figures deep in the twilight mist moving gracefully across the swamp, singing with voices like those of angels. The Okefenokeee Swamp might have relinquished most of its mysteries, but it seems that there is one that will continue to confound and to puzzle.

Brown Mountain Lights
BURKE COUNTY, NORTH CAROLINA

Northern and southern lights, aurora borealis and aurora australis respectively, are wisps of seemingly ethereal light fluttering and flickering across the star-lit sky in varying shades of blues, greens and reds. The phenomena are most intense near the north and south poles but also occur in other parts of the northern and southern hemispheres. Those living in the continental United States might live their whole lives without ever bearing witness to the brilliant spectacle, but the people of Burke County, North Carolina, are often treated to their own spectacular light show radiating from the foothills of the Blue Ridge, atop the long and low Brown Mountain.

The lights have been seen for centuries, moving up and down across the night sky, illuminated orbs of blue and red that rise thick and fast from the horizon. The explanations for the eerie lights that move across Brown Mountain are many and varied. Some have their roots in science, while others use hypotheses less empirical but no less persuasive. Are the Brown Mountain Lights evidence of an underground alien base, of another Roswell, New Mexico? Are the lights the spirit of a corpse found at the foot of the mountain? Whatever their origins, these lights stun and awe all those who gaze upon them. So pervasive has the phenomenon been over the years that even the U.S. Geological Survey has tried to solve its mysteries. But those who have attempted to do so learn that the Brown Lights do not give up the answers to their riddles so easily.

The Cherokee Indians, who populated these lands before European explorers usurped them, looked upon the lights with a religious reverence. Gathered upon the hills around Brown Mountain, the Cherokee would tell their youth the story of the great battle of 1200. When the battle had come to an end, the air was thick and heavy with the smell of blood and the incessant buzzing of flies. Walking this field at the time were those who couldn't fight—women, children and elders—and those who wouldn't fight—medicine men and shamans. Families walked about, torches in hand, searching for loved ones and relations. The flies scattered ahead of them, and the buzzing gave way to wails of anger and loss. Women and children collapsed next to the bodies of husbands, fathers, uncles and brothers. Medicine men applied poultices made from plants on the wounds of the crippled and the weak, applying centuries-old knowledge in the desperate attempt to prevent further death. The devastation was almost too much to bear as the dead were wrapped in their burial shrouds and interred.

The losses scarred the tribe and their land. Even after the rain washed away the blood, the field still resonated with the whispers of the dead. It was there that the eerie lights rose above the ridge of the Brown Mountain, moving back and forth across the horizon. Today, Cherokee looking at these lights cannot help remembering the mournful battle their ancestors fought so many years ago. Cherokee lore states that the lights of the Brown Mountain are lingering remnants of the spirits of the Indian maidens who walked the fields seeking their loved ones.

Just as the Cherokee nation fell from prominence in the wake of European colonization, so too did their beliefs about the Brown Mountain Lights. While the earliest colonials shared the Cherokee's beliefs, it wasn't long before the rational minds of the Europeans rejected the idea of the paranormal in favor of more quantifiable evidence.

In 1771, German engineer Gerard William de Brahm was intrigued by the phenomenon. He had yet to witness it for himself, but he had heard it described so many times that his curiosity was piqued. A man of science, de Brahm had been approached by a number of people hoping he could provide an explanation for the lights that appeared on moonless autumn nights. De Brahm set out for Wiseman's View on Linville Mountain, where it was said the lights could be best seen. He'd heard how people believed that the lights were something supernatural and beyond the physical world, but he thought that was all rubbish. It was an age of reason and he would find a concrete explanation.

Applying his knowledge of gas and combustion, de Brahm came to the conclusion that the mountains were spewing out gaseous vapors that became airborne, carried by the wind. When one breeze met another, the resulting friction caused the vapors to ignite, resulting in the bursts of light up and down along the ridge. As the years passed, de Brahm's theory was proven to be invalid; there were no nitrous vapors, as he called them, escaping from the earth. In his quest to suffuse the Brown Mountain Lights with reason, he ended up offering an explanation grounded not in the cold and hard facts of science, but in the murk and fog of speculation.

For years after, some accepted de Brahm's ideas as a suitable explanation, while others provided their own reasons for the Brown Mountain Lights. A number of ideas sprang up and were spread from generation to generation within communities, much like homemade remedies for the common cold. In the early 20th century the local phenomenon attracted enough national attention to merit a study by the U.S. Geological Survey.

The organization's scientists came to North Carolina in 1913, armed with the latest in monitoring equipment and a determination to uncover the lights' mysteries. After a few days of surveying and measurements, they decided that the Brown Mountain Lights were little more than the distortion of something very common and ordinary. There was nothing unusual at work here except maybe some of the laws of physics. The lights were nothing more than locomotive headlights approaching from the Catawba Valley to the south. Of course, the scientists neglected one little detail. They ignored the fact that

Cherokee Indians had seen the lights long before the locomotive ever came to North Carolina. And when, in 1916,
a flood roared and crashed its way through the Catawba
Valley, the railroad bridges buckled and quivered before
giving way. Repairs took weeks, during which time it was
impossible for trains to cross the valley. Strangely enough,
though, the Brown Mountain Lights continued to flicker
and dance.

A doctor with the U.S. Weather Bureau was also asked
to investigate the lights. Dr. Humphries was not surprised
by the spectacle, thinking that the Brown Mountain
Lights reminded him very much of other light-related
phenomena such as St. Elmo's Fire and the Andes Lights
in South America. St. Elmo's Fire is a scientifically accepted
occurrence, and has been described by Julius Caesar,
William Shakespeare and Herman Melville. The lights are
usually seen around projections, such as chimneys and
church spires, before or after a thunderstorm. Atoms are
stripped of electrons, creating the bright spheres of light.
Regardless, Dr. Humphries could not explain why the
Brown Mountain Lights might be seen on days where the
skies were clear and when there had been no thunder-
storms.

By the 1960s, a small population believed they had
uncovered the roots of the Brown Mountain Lights. Ralph
Lael, a shop owner who worked near the area, claimed
that aliens abducted him in 1962 and that the Brown
Mountain Lights are the lights from UFOs. The ridge is
apparently a landing pad for extraterrestrial visitors, and
the mountains themselves may hide an underground alien
base. Lael believed the extraterrestrials landed here to

gather information about earth life before taking off to return to their unknown origins. Lael claimed to have been abducted a number of times from the Brown Mountain. During one of his trips aboard a UFO, he was able to obtain what he called an alien mummy, a figure about 3 to 4 feet high. The figure had obviously walked upright and had four limbs just like humans, but there the similarities ended. Its face was something from a dream, with features that could have been human but were undeniably foreign in origin.

For years, Lael displayed the figure in a glass coffin in his Outer Space Rock Shop Museum on Highway 181 outside Morganton. He dismissed any other explanations for the Brown Mountain Lights, suggesting that any theories were just smoke screens, variations on a theme of deception and signs of a vast conspiracy perpetrated to keep the existence of extraterrestrial life secret. Conspiracy theorists who rallied around Lael during his lifetime rallied once again around the former congressional candidate in death. They found it suspicious that after Lael died, the alien mummy that he had displayed so proudly in his museum disappeared under mysterious circumstances. It is still missing, yet still the lights rise on crisp autumn nights, igniting curiosities.

Those who have grown up around the phenomenon have been told stories about the lights from the first time the lights fired their imaginations. Tragedy lies at the core of most of these theories, like the story of the dedicated slave who wandered out into the mountains to search for his master. The slave knew the land well, and took with him only some provisions and a lamp to light his way. Of course, his master knew the land well too, and survival in the wilderness had been part of his training when he joined the Confederate Army. So when neither the master nor the slave returned, people wondered what had happened on the mountain to swallow them up. The two bodies never were found, but the lights on the Brown Mountain might very well be the lamps of the phantom master and slave trying to find their way off the mountain.

In the end, the lights represent something different for everyone. Whether they are just an unexplained natural phenomenon, the spiritual remnants of people whose lives were all too brief or signs of intelligent life somewhere else in the universe, the one guarantee of the Brown Mountain Lights is that they will continue to inspire awe and wonder in those who chance to glance upon them. In a world where things change at the speed of light, there is something reassuring about being able to glance upon lights that have illuminated the land for centuries. Like the stars, the sun and the moon, they connect the present with the past and stand as symbols of the beautiful and marvelous in the surrounding world.

8

An Assortment of Spooks

Castle Hill Mansion
CASTLE HILL, VIRGINIA

Dr. Thomas Walker rose out of bed. The knocking at his front door was loud and insistent. Walker should have been upset, but he wasn't. It was a time of war, and colonials had come often to his house in Castle Hill, Virginia, seeking shelter or supplies. He walked to the door with a lit lantern, and as he opened the door he drew back in fear. Standing before him, wreathed in the flickering shadows of candlelight, was a giant of a man, eyes wild with desperation, face bloodied.

Walker soon learned that the man in front of him was Jack Jouett, a captain in the Virginia militia. Jouett was on a mission that might win the colonials their freedom; he had already ridden 40 miles that night, through thick forest where branches had torn at his face. His horse was nearly dead with exhaustion. He asked Dr. Walker for a fresh mount so that he might speed his journey to Monticello, where he needed to get word to Thomas Jefferson and 40 members of the legislature to flee the city ahead of the advancing British. As he leaped upon his fresh steed, he asked the doctor for one more favor.

"If they stop here," Jouett said, "delay them. Delay them for as long as you can. My journey depends upon it."

Dr. Walker gave his word and watched Jouett disappear into the darkness. He then rushed into his home, woke his wife and began to prepare for the soldiers' arrival.

Colonel Banastre Tarleton and his men arrived a short time later, just as the rosy tendrils of the morning sun crept across the horizon. Tarleton dismounted and demanded that Dr. Walker provide him and his men with food.

Dr. Walker and his wife welcomed the redcoats into their home. Their cook had already been warned to delay the preparation of the soldiers' meals for as long as possible. While the men waited, the Walkers served the men round upon round of heavily spiked mint juleps, hoping to dull their senses. The ruse worked, if for just a while. But Tarleton, despite the warm flush he felt that often accompanies slight inebriation, was not a feared colonel because he was unobservant. He stormed into the kitchen, demanding to know why the food was so long in coming. The cooks pleaded ignorance. Tarleton slammed a fist on a table, demanded no more delays and then turned abruptly to leave the kitchen.

The food was served, and soon the men made ready to ride. Walker tried to delay the men, offering them more food and asking them if they wouldn't like to rest for a little while longer. Tarleton politely, but firmly, refused all such entreaties. And then Dr. Walker's wife approached the colonel.

"Colonel," she said, "your road is long and it is hard. You have already traveled so far and to such lengths. Surely, there must be something else here that you want. The constant company of men, here in a strange and foreign land, could not possibly be fulfilling."

Tarleton paused, asking his men to halt. It had been far too long since he had experienced the soft and delicate touch of a woman.

"We will stay here a while longer."

Hours passed before the colonel emerged from the house. When he did, he ordered the men to move and he followed, saluting the good doctor and his wife and thanking them for their hospitality.

To their great relief, the Walkers learned that Jouett had managed to reach Monticello with his message. Jefferson and the 40 members of legislature, among them Patrick Henry, Thomas Lee and Benjamin Harrison, had fled the city, spiriting away Tarleton's prize. Jouett's ride, Dr. Walker's manipulation and his wife's offer had saved Thomas Jefferson from capture. And while the spirits of Jouett and Walker departed this earth long ago, the house on Castle Hill remains, standing as a testament to their courage. And so too might Walker's wife.

Walker first built this stately residence in 1764, inviting such luminaries as James Madison and Thomas Jefferson to grace its halls. The wooden structure he erected, however, proved not to be the most durable, and in 1823, then-owner William Cabel Rives, a US senator and Confederate congressman, used brick to augment and bolster the sagging wooden frames. Rives was decadent, and the home reflected his tastes; brick was imported from England, glass and other fixtures came from London. He erected a row of Tuscan Doric columns to run the length of the house.

While Rives lived there, he never experienced anything out of the ordinary. It wasn't until his granddaughter, novelist Amelie Rives, had taken possession of the house that Castle Hill's haunted history began. Married to Russian painter Pierre Troubetzkoy, Rives was a prominent social figure who enjoyed entertaining guests and friends and members of the social elite. Overnight guests were common at Castle Hill, and it was they who first experienced phenomena that could not be explained.

Over breakfast, guests would complain to their hosts about how they were unable to sleep, that they had been kept awake all night by the noise of someone climbing up and down the staircase. Voices loud enough to raise the dead (ironically enough, it was probably the dead who were speaking), woke others from sleep. Yet when the perturbed guests left their rooms to investigate the conversations they heard just outside their doors, there was no one to be found.

Amelie herself was often assailed by the smell of a perfume she had never worn. When guests asked her where she bought that beautiful rose-scented water, Amelie would know that Castle Hill's permanent resident had paid a visit.

As the years passed, the ghost grew bolder. A former housekeeper at the house described how someone would grab her leg anytime she slept without covers; she blamed the events on the ghost. And guests staying in what would become known as the pink bedroom reported frequent disturbances at the hands of a young pretty woman, at times playful, at other times frightening. Strangely, though, some guests slept in the pink bedroom without interruption. The belief is that the pretty young ghost is selective with the people she chooses to disturb, and that should you strike her fancy, your stay will be one of blissful ease.

Skeptical writer Julian Green, who steadfastly denied the existence of ghosts, stayed in the pink bedroom one evening. He fled the home sometime during the evening without even bidding farewell to his hosts. Never did he discuss what had happened, and the reasons for his departure went with him to his grave when Green died in 1998. Of course, one can hazard a guess as to what happened. After all, Green was not the only guest to flee Castle Hill. One described how a beautiful woman, dressed in clothing the likes of which hadn't been seen in almost two centuries, had woken him up and then whispered in his ear that he had to go. The incident unnerved the man fully and whenever he was asked to discuss his experience, he became incoherent and shook his arms in the air. Apparently, Green was one of those of whom the ghost didn't approve.

No one is sure who this female ghost is, but to be sure, she has the final say in who gets to sleep in what must have once been her bedroom. Some speculate that the pretty apparition is the reincarnation of Dr. Walker's wife. The ghost's clothing appears to match the fashions of the late 18th century, and as one of the house's original tenants, Mrs. Walker may believe that she still has the authority to decide who is allowed to stay at her house. And why not? It is her right. Without her, the British Colonel Tarleton might have succeeded in his quest to capture Thomas Jefferson and bring the colonials to their knees.

The Johnstone Legacy
MADISON, MISSISSIPPI

The Johnstones had been a distinguished family with a proud name centuries before they emigrated to the United States. First appearing in Scottish lore and history in 1214, the Johnstones were a family of wealth and prominence who played central roles in both the defense of Scotland and its union with Great Britain. They owned much land, carving out luxury and opulence from the wilderness in Annandale. The fertile lands became known as the Barony of Johnstone. Before the technological advances of the Industrial Revolution, land was central to wealth and prestige. In a society based upon agriculture, fertile soil was essential, and the Johnstones had acres of it.

By the 18th century, even their extensive holdings could not satisfy the vast number of Johnstones who had grown exponentially with each generation. Some decided that opportunities in the land of the thistle had been exhausted and looked westward across the Atlantic to the land of opportunity: the British colonies in North America. Stories of how colonials had been able to build grand plantations to harvest profitable crops like cotton, tobacco and sorghum were written boldly in the cargo-laden ships that arrived in Britain from the Americas. Some of the more enterprising Johnstones decided to test their mettle in America and emigrated there.

The Johnstones settled in Bertie County, North Carolina, and soon enjoyed the same degree of affluence, power and influence as they had in Scotland. A century later, John T. Johnstone, the great-grandson of one of the original emigres, set out for the west again. Lands there had been cleared of the Indian presence to be brought under the till and hoe of European settlers.

John and two of his brothers traveled to Mississippi. Once there, they set about acquiring acres upon acres of land. In 1835, John, determined to do his family name proud and create a lasting legacy, bought the first 520 acres of what would eventually become a 2500-acre plantation just southeast of Livingston. He could not have known that in buying the land, he had set in motion supernatural forces that would cement the Johnstone reputation, though quite possibly not in the manner he had envisioned. He could not have known that after his death, the plantation he called Annandale in honor of his ancestral home would dwindle away with nothing but ruins and some ghosts to mark his presence.

In 1840 John and his wife, Margaret, moved from North Carolina to Mississippi along with their children, Frances and Helen. They lived in a log cabin that had come with John's original purchase of the 520 acres. To accommodate the family, the cabin was enlarged while their house, Ingleside, was being built.

When Frances married in 1844, John gave her 1400 acres adjacent to Annandale as a wedding gift. Then in 1848, when John died suddenly, Margaret took over control of the family business. But crucial to her was the fulfillment of John's plans. Before his death, he had spoken often about the construction of two buildings: one

Still mourning the loss of her true love, the ghost of Helen Johnstone haunts the Chapel of the Cross in Madison, Mississippi.

would be a house of worship, the other a house of spectacle.

In 1848, Margaret employed a small fleet of artisans and plantation laborers to build the church. Set in a glade, the church was placed in the shadows of the trees that lined the lands: magnolia, oak and cedar. Rafters and sills in the church were hewn from the sturdy trees that had grown for centuries upon the plantation, and Italian stone was imported to complete the church's baptismal font. In 1852 the Chapel of the Cross was consecrated.

Seven years later, Margaret was able to move into the newly constructed Annandale house. Here, Margaret and her children entertained many guests. The grand staircase, the centerpiece of the 40-room, three-story mansion, was large enough to hold a full orchestra that encouraged dancing across two hardwood floors. Rooms were heated from fires that burned in the carved marble fireplaces imported from Europe. John no doubt would have been pleased with all Margaret had done both to honor and to realize his dreams. His daughter was not as fortunate to have found such a spouse.

Helen's life was tragic. In 1857, she fell in love with Henry Vick, the son of the founder of Vicksburg, and the couple planned to be married on Helen's birthday. But for reasons unknown, Henry Vick rode out to New Orleans just four days before the wedding to take part in a duel, thereby placing himself under God's judgment. While the practice of dueling was outlawed, it was still viewed as an integral component of life in the South. For Southern gentlemen, it was the only means of preserving honor and righting certain inequities. On the appointed day, Vick drew a pistol and rode out to the dueling grounds. The Lord must have judged Vick in the wrong, for he was slain with a single bullet to the heart. As his life pumped out of him, Vick gasped and uttered the name of his betrothed. It was the last word he ever spoke.

The news devastated Helen. On her birthday, it was not a wedding that took place in the Chapel of the Cross, but a funeral procession. Dressed in black, Helen stood before Vick's casket and kissed the polished wood. She knew then that she would always love him. His casket was led by torchlight to the family cemetery where he was buried. Helen spent endless hours sitting by the tombstone and weeping.

While her heart would always truly belong to Henry Vick, Helen eventually married another. George Harris was a rector who worked at the Chapel of the Cross. Harris was aware that she could never love him fully, and while he originally believed that he could adapt to that reality, as the years passed, he found himself growing more and more possessive. The idea of it haunted him, for he was a man of the cloth, a man who should be beyond the frailties of men. Yet there he was, jealous of a dead man, possessed of the knowledge that there was no possible way he could ever compete with a man who would forever remain perfect in his wife's eyes. When Helen died, her will revealed that she wanted to be buried next to Henry Vick, so that the two might be united in death forever. Harris refused to allow it to happen and she was buried in another cemetery, far from her beloved. Love, however, will find a way.

In death, Helen Johnstone has returned to the Chapel of the Cross. It is her apparition visitors report seeing, sitting on an iron bench next to a tombstone bearing the name Henry Vick, her shoulders hunched in misery. The world around her has changed, yet she remains a constant in Madison County, Mississippi. Generations of children have come and gone, each whispering about the ghost at the Chapel of the Cross. Senior high school students use her presence to initiate freshmen. All the while, Helen mourns her true love's death.

Henry Vick's passing was the first in a line of tragedies that saw the precipitous fall of the Johnstone empire. In 1860, with the secession of South Carolina from the United States, the Civil War began; hanging in the balance was the antebellum South in which the Johnstones had gathered their wealth. After the war, when the Confederacy lay in ruins and slavery had been eliminated with the Emancipation Proclamation, the economy of the South changed dramatically.

Without free labor and slaves to work the plantation, the fortunes of the Annandale plantation were quickly depleted. Margaret did what she could to adapt to the new economy but still found herself in the unenviable position of selling off the plantation acre by acre. Her staff of faithful servants chose to stick by her, and one in particular, Annie Devlin, worked tirelessly in her dedication to Margaret and Annandale. Annie Devlin had promised Margaret during the Civil War that she would never leave and it seems as if she really meant it.

Annie Devlin died at the dawn of the 20th century but her spirit stayed behind, answering doors for guests, walking the halls and frightening those who chose to sleep in her old bedroom. More than one of Margaret's guests would entertain her with stories of sleepless nights, of the apparition that continued to pull their covers from them. Margaret could only shake her head and reassure her guests that the spirit meant no harm.

The Johnstone heritage slowly faded; Margaret died in 1880, Helen passed on in 1916 and in 1924, Annandale Mansion burned down. It's said that while the mansion burned, Annie Devlin appeared in a second-floor window, wrapped in a shawl, wondering what all the commotion was about. But the home that Margaret had built to honor her husband was lost forever. For a time, it seemed as if the Chapel of the Cross would follow suit.

Following the Civil War, the Chapel of the Cross became obsolete and few came to worship there. By the turn of the century, the Diocese of Mississippi had declared the church extinct, and it stood abandoned and neglected. Margaret Britton Parsons saved the church when she petitioned the Episcopal Diocese of Mississippi successfully to reconsecrate the Chapel of the Cross. This task was done and thus the church was saved. One wonders what would have happened to Helen had the building been razed; with its preservation and its place on the National Register of Historic Places, the Gothic Revival church continues to serve the public with four services every Sunday. It also serves as the backdrop for the ongoing drama of Helen Johnstone's sad life.

Haunted Hunter
CHARLESTON, SOUTH CAROLINA

Maria Heyward was confused. She had come into the library because she'd heard a noise, which was strange because she was supposed to be alone in the house her mother had built in Charleston, South Carolina. In the orange glow of the rising sun, Maria could make out the shape of a man sitting in a wing-back chair in front of the fireplace. The man was asleep, his feet up on an ottoman, head sagging towards his chest. Shielding her eyes from the brightening of the sun, she saw that it was her brother, James, asleep in the chair. How odd, she thought to herself. Hadn't he left earlier that morning with some friends so they could spend the day hunting deer? Not that it mattered. Perhaps he changed his mind. For there he was, sunken into the chair, still dressed in his hunting clothes, clothes soiled from the field. On his head sat a pea-green felt cap. Maria crept out of the library, careful not to wake her slumbering brother. She would remind him later that he, the consummate gentleman, had forgotten to take off his hat in the house.

Easing the door shut behind her, Maria went about the rest of her day as she always did. She finished up the chores her mother had asked her to do, sweeping the halls, dusting the windowsills, wiping down tabletops and windows. Standing in the front hall, surveying her work, Maria allowed herself a small nod of satisfaction before a commotion from outside caught her attention. She opened the front door and saw that the hunting party had returned.

The apparition of James Heyward appears in the library of his former home in Charleston, South Carolina.

The men bore the vacant and blank stares of the grief-stricken. Some of the men's dirty faces were streaked with tears, the drops having carved tiny rivulets through the mud and dust. Maria's smile faded when her gaze fell upon the slumped figure tethered to his mount. The body was slack, pitched forward over the horse as if all life had been drained from it. The head was obscured with blood-soaked fabric, but Maria didn't need to see the head to know that she was looking at the lifeless body of her brother. The coat was unmistakably his. She ran from the porch into the house, pursued by her older brother, who had also been part of the hunting party. He held her closely and told her what happened between her muffled sobs.

The hunting trip turned for the worse when James, the lead rider, took the party down an old hunting trail. Wide at its origins, the trail became progressively narrower, encroached on both sides by thick hedges. The hunting dogs worked the trail, trying to sniff out something for their masters to shoot. Unfortunately, all they did was set in motion the events that led to James' death.

Their barking had startled a wild boar, which came snarling and snorting down the path. The dogs tried to hold their ground until the wild creature began thrashing about with its tusks. The barks became whimpers and the dogs turned to retreat. But alas, they had nowhere to go on the narrow trail. Having first spooked the boar, they now frightened James' horse as they ran in and around the animal's legs. The horse whinnied, raising itself on its two hind legs. James tried to steady his mount, but the dogs, now frenzied, continued to move in and out around the horse.

Desperate, James drew his rifle and began to beat both dog and boar with the butt of his gun. It was a foolish tactic that discharged a bullet straight into James' head. His body was launched from the horse and the party could only watch as James crashed lifeless to the ground.

"When did this awful thing happen?" Maria whispered.

"Early this morning," her brother replied.

Maria broke free from the comfort of her brother's grasp. She shook her head.

"That's impossible," Maria said. "Why, just this morning I saw James asleep in the library. He must be alive."

Her brother stated that his sister must be mistaken. James had left with the hunting party early in the morning and had led the party the entire time. He couldn't have left. Indeed, the retort of the gun that killed his brother still echoed in his mind and it would be years before the image of his kin flying through the air would lose its impact and immediacy. He drew a deep breath and held his sister close. He asked her when she had seen him. She answered at eight in the morning.

"Maria," the brother said. "Eight o'clock is the hour when James was shot."

Maria shook her head, incredulous. Her mind struggled to reconcile the incongruities of the facts as they lay before her. She was sure she had seen James in the library that morning. Her brother was equally sure of what he had seen. But standing there, as the wind blew through the open door, she began to feel the bluntness of the truth. The man inside the library might have looked like James, but the more she thought about it, the more she realized he was more doppelganger than genuine article. She remembered that she hadn't spoken to him and that he was surprisingly quiet while asleep even though he was notorious for his snore. She noted that he would never wear muddy shoes into the house and, most of all, that he was too much the gentleman to enter the house with his hat on. Her body sagged.

"Our brother is dead," she whispered through tears.

The Heyward family was devastated by the loss. They lived the rest of their days haunted by the lost possibilities of what James might have been and might have done. He had lived so few precious years and now all the Heywards had were memories. But there is life after death, or at least there was for James.

James died in 1805. Years later, in the late 19th century, people who moved into 31 Legare Street soon realized that they were not alone in the two-and-a-half-story wooden house. No matter what happened to the library where Maria had seen her brother, regardless of whether it became a den or a dining room, there was always one constant. James Heyward, unfortunate hunting victim, still uses the room as his library.

He has been seen on a number of occasions in the room, although gone are the muddy clothes and boots. He is a resplendent spirit; his hair is immaculately groomed, with no hat in sight. Meditative and contemplative, James is seen standing by the window, staring out into the distance. Now and again, he will pull his gaze away from the window and turn his eyes to the book that he always has in hand, reading for a few minutes and then turning back to the view. When he turns to walk out of the room, he disappears into shadow. Perhaps he is able to make up in the afterlife what he missed out on in life.

Gardette-Le Pretre House
NEW ORLEANS, LOUISIANA

Jean Baptiste Le Pretre had a problem. His fortunes were dwindling. At one time, La Prete was among the wealthiest of New Orleans' Creoles. He was a towering and imposing figure of prestige and power. His home, built in 1836 in the French Quarter, was the architectural embodiment of his stature. Even in a neighborhood famed for its grand mansions, Le Pretre's home towered above them in size, luxury and opulence. He may not have been the one to build the home, but he was the one who had the means to maintain it. Most homes on Dauphine Street operated a business on the ground floor, while the living quarters were stationed above. Le Pretre, the wealthy planter and banker, was able to convert the whole of it all into a monument to opulence. But as it was with so many of the Creole families of New Orleans, wealth and fortunes were fleeting.

And now, Le Pretre sat in his stately study, looking over his bank ledgers, wondering how in the world his wealth had dwindled to almost nothing. He didn't have the resources to last another year if something weren't done to rectify the situation. He'd already sold off most of his assets, but it still wasn't enough.

He walked around his mansion, wondering what else he had that could be made to turn a profit. His fingers ran along the fine grain of the highly polished wooden banister of his grand staircase and as they did, he hit upon an idea. It wasn't the best idea, and the very fact that he was

The Gardette-Le Pretre House in New Orleans, Louisiana

even thinking it only reminded him of how far he had fallen. But what else could he do?

His greatest asset was still his mansion. But he refused to sell it. He couldn't. It would mean defeat, and Le Pretre still had some fight left in him. He decided to become a landlord instead. From the moment the first cornerstone of the building had been laid, he had hoped that the mansion would be passed down through generation after generation of his family, but that dream was impossible now.

He began the process of finding the proper tenant, and after weeks of what he thought was a rigorous screening process, he settled upon a man who had claimed to be a Turkish sultan. He'd left Turkey, it was said, because he had acquired some very powerful enemies who wanted him dead. So the young Turk had fled to America, his trip bankrolled by part of the vast fortune in gold that he'd brought with him. It's said that it took days just to transport his wealth from the docks to the banks.

Le Pretre was impressed with the Turk's wealth, and, as a banker, welcomed the business. He handed the young man the keys for the house, a decision that he would later come to regret. The sultan made little effort to blend in with his environment. Even in a city as flamboyant as New Orleans, the Turk stood out.

Using the vast reserves of wealth at his disposal, the sultan made every effort to remake the mansion to resemble those found in his native land. He also spared no expense for his protection; a small army of men with scimitars walked the locked and gated grounds at all hours of the day, allowing entrance only to the sultan's harem of women and Arab boys. Neighbors could only speculate as to what went on in the mansion, their imaginations fueled by the strange music that could be heard from behind the darkened windows. But then came the day that everything stopped.

Several grisly murders occurred in the house while it was rented out by a wealthy Turkish sultan.

The house fell silent. There were no cries or loud music, and the sweet scent of incense that used to hang thickly in the air had been replaced with the smell of something else altogether. It was the scent of blood, and residents noticed that it came from the streams of red liquid that were running out from the mansion in rivulets and pooling on the streets.

Authorities were called in. The gates were broken down. And the crowds gathered on the street, craning their heads this way and that for a look inside the house. Even the hardened policemen who had been dealing with death and mayhem for years were finding it difficult to keep their stomachs from lurching at what they found in the mansion. No one knows who was responsible for the crime, but at some point during the previous evening, everyone inside the house had been killed. Their limbs were severed and strewn throughout the mansion. It was impossible to know which limb belonged to which body. It seemed, for a moment, that perhaps there was a survivor. No one seemed able to find the head or body of the young sultan. It was hoped that he had escaped.

The hope was futile. When policemen searched the yard of the mansion, they found a fresh grave under a date tree. Upon exhumation, they found the dismembered body of the sultan. The tree bore an inscription, proclaiming that "the justice of heaven is satisfied, and the date tree shall grow on the traitor's tomb." Not surprisingly, the tree was known forever afterward as the Death Tree.

The French Quarter buzzed with rumor and speculation. What had happened to the sultan? Who could have done such a thing? What could have possibly motivated such a heinous act? Was it a political assassination? Had the sultan managed to anger the wrong people, perhaps vengeful pirates who were known to kill without hesitation? Or had the sultan fled Turkey because he was thief,

Today, apparitions of the dead sultan and other victims continue to terrify tenants.

because he had robbed his own family of their hard-earned wealth? No one ever uncovered the truth, but for years after, the crime was unforgettable in its horror and terror. It helped, too, that the mansion still clings to the past tenaciously.

Although the Le Pretre Mansion was converted into apartments long ago, the house is still legendary not only for the gruesome murders that took place within its walls, but also for its hauntings. Though dead, the sultan and the other victims still inhabit the mansion and it doesn't seem as if they have allowed even death to interrupt their lifestyles. Their forms still walk the halls and up and down the staircases of the mansion, their apparitions accompanied always by the strains of music that were first heard when the sultan began renting Le Pretre's mansion. It's only at night that the nightmares begin, when the sun has sunk beneath the horizon and the air is still. Tenants reported being roused from sleep by a host of screams, a multitude of voices calling out for help in desperation and then complete silence.

Enjoy more terrifying tales in these collections by

GHOST HOUSE BOOKS

The colorful history of North America includes many spine-tingling tales of the supernatural. These fun, fascinating collections from GHOST HOUSE BOOKS involve well-known homes, public buildings and prominent landmarks, many of which are still in use. Collect the whole series!

Haunted Houses *by Edrick Thay*
With their blend of captivating history and ethereal residents, haunted houses have long been considered the most exciting haunted places. This eagerly awaited collection reveals why.
$10.95US/$14.95CDN • ISBN 1-894877-30-6 • 5.25" x 8.25" • 256 pages

Ghost Stories of Civil War *by Dan Asfar and Edrick Thay*
In this new collection, authors Dan Asfar and Edrick Thay recount fascinating stories of soldiers, statesmen and star-crossed lovers, both ordinary and extraordinary, whose lingering spirits serve as a testament to America's most devastating war.
$10.95US/$14.95CDN • ISBN 1-894877-16-0 • 5.25" x 8.25" • 216 pages

Ghost Stories of America, Volume 2 *by A.S. Mott*
Covering every region and era, A.S. Mott explores the nation's most infamous spirits, paranormal phenomena and haunted places, making this collection essential reading for skeptics and believers alike.
$10.95US/$14.95CDN • ISBN 1-894877-31-4 • 5.25" x 8.25" • 248 pages

Ghost Stories of the Old West *by Dan Asfar*
The OK Corral, Fort Leavenworth, Billy the Kid, the Pony Express—the Old West had it all. Join Dan Asfar as he uncovers the charismatic ghosts who inhabit the prisons, forts and saloons where the Old West was born—and died.
$10.95US/$14.95CDN • ISBN 1-894877-17-9 • 5.25" x 8.25" • 216 pages

Also look for
Ghost Stories of America *by Dan Asfar and Edrick Thay*   ISBN 1-894877-11-X
Campfire Ghost Stories *by Jo-Anne Christensen*   ISBN 1-894877-02-0
Haunted Theaters *by Barbara Smith*   ISBN 1-894877-04-7

These and many more Ghost House books are available from your local bookseller or by ordering direct. In the U.S., call 1-800-518-3541. In Canada, call 1-800-661-9017.